THE BATTLES OF WORLD WAR I:
Everything You Need to Know

CHRISTOPHER CATHERWOOD

Allison & Busby Limited
12 Fitzroy Mews
London W1T 6DW
www.allisonandbusby.com

First published in Great Britain by Allison & Busby in 2014.

A CIP catalogue record for this book is available from
the British Library.

First Edition

ISBN 978-0-7490-1596-1

Typeset in 11.75/16.75 pt Sabon by
Allison & Busby Ltd.

The paper used for this Allison & Busby publication
has been produced from trees that have been legally sourced
from well-managed and credibly certified forests.

Printed and bound by
CPI Group (UK) Ltd, Croydon, CR0 4YY

To the memory of my great-uncle
Harold Lloyd-Jones
1898–1918,
who never saw the Allied victory,
and to his wonderful great-niece-in-law,
my wife Paulette

TABLE OF CONTENTS

PART FIVE: THE ROAD TO FINAL VICTORY

FOREWORD

The year 2014 heralds the centenary of the beginning of perhaps the most important war in history. Because of World War I many of the extraordinary events and creations of the twentieth century came about. Outstanding examples would include: the Russian Revolution, the rise of Nazism, World War II, the origins of the state of Israel and the creation of several new countries without regard for ethnic mix or ancient rivalries.

Many excellent books have been published recently to begin the commemorative process for this landmark centenary event. Most of them have one thing in common – they are substantial in length. Some of these books, such as those by Max Hastings and Margaret MacMillan, also take us no further than the end of 1914. If they were to cover the whole war they would be several volumes. This is indeed the case for the series that Professor Hew Strachan at Oxford University is now writing.

What, though, if you want just a straightforward overview of some of the key battles of World War I? In an ideal world we would have time to read long books, but in practice there is always a place for something shorter and more succinct. This book aims to fulfil the quest for the latter: a work that gives the key battles and their outcomes in nutshell form.

Brevity, of course, means that some things need to be left out. Regimental histories are great at telling us what brave lieutenant or sergeant accomplished what heroic feat, but with battles containing hundreds of thousands of troops from dozens of regiments, such microscopic detail becomes impossible. Thankfully the Imperial War Museum believed from early on in oral history. The memories and letters of countless British soldiers are not only there to inspect but have been published as well. Precise accounts of individual regimental movements down to unit level are best left to such works. But the bigger picture is also important, and the interpretation and significance of the various confrontations lie at the heart of this particular book.

Inevitably some memorable battles have also had to be omitted. Much of the war in Flanders and northern France from late 1914 until the summer of 1918 consisted of futile attempts by the British and French to batter through German lines. Millions of soldiers died in the horror of the trenches, in the attempt to gain but a few yards of enemy land. And the outcome of many of these battles, each one seen at the time as being so vitally important for the descendants of those who took part in them, sadly ended up being just as fruitless. Only the truly epic clashes such as the Somme or Passchendaele stand out, often, tragically, because of the sheer scale of the carnage involved.

In addition, I have not given details of the Home Front, which has been ably documented in a recent book by Jeremy Paxman. In concentrating on individual battles I have mentioned their context, so some of the background wider history of the war does come in through that route.

Some other issues are important to note.

Firstly, no one ever seems to agree on precise casualty figures. Even standard works disagree with each other, and one of these, by Correlli Barnett, shows that this can sometimes lead to discrepancies of several *million* deaths. The figures for Britain and its colonies tend to be somewhat more precise, but the reporting of German and Russian figures can differ wildly. Wikipedia is tremendously helpful as a starting point. However, some of the details there need to be checked against other statistics for a different point of view.

Secondly, town names change, and sometimes have

changed more than once. St Petersburg briefly became Petrograd, then Leningrad for many years before becoming St Petersburg again. Towns in German Poland changed their names, as did cities in Austrian-ruled Galicia or Bohemia. I have tried to use the name that was employed at that time.

Finally, it is important to emphasise that, if we are to get a balanced picture of the *whole* war, we need to look beyond the Western Front. Communism came to power as a result of the stalemate on the *Eastern* Front. So desperate were the Germans to get Russia out of the war that they sent Lenin back home from exile in Switzerland. The plot worked. The Communists under Lenin took power and withdrew from the conflict. But the world then had seventy-four years of the USSR. During that time millions were killed by the secret police. What became the Cold War lasted from the 1940s down to more recent times.

This book is being written against the backdrop of acute conflict in the Middle East. Many attribute this tragically fairly normal state of affairs to the creation of Israel in 1948. But with no British capture of Jerusalem in 1917 there would have been no Israel to create thirty-one years later. Similarly, without the capture of Damascus in 1918 there might have been no Syria in existence to have a civil war in our own time.

This is an overview, therefore, of battles on both Eastern and Western Fronts. By and large I have not given many eyewitness accounts, since these are readily available in much longer books listed in the bibliography, online through the BBC or Imperial War Museum. Maps are a necessary aide to understanding the geography of war. Today's interactive online maps are superior to classic static ones. The bibliography lists some of the more helpful of these. This work is, if you like, a starter course, designed to whet the appetite for people to gain the aerial photograph view of the war and its causes. The results of World War I are still with us a century later, so that is the focus of much of our book. It looks not just at the key battles of long ago, but at the impact that they have had on the world we live in today.

INTRODUCTION

HOW WAR BEGAN

CHANGING PERSPECTIVES

In Flanders fields the poppies blow
Between the crosses, row on row

'In Flanders Fields' (1915) by John McCrae, probably the best-known poem of the First World War, reminds us all too vividly of the horrors of that conflict. To the poet's images we can add men sitting in trenches preparing to go 'over the top', cratered landscapes resembling the moon, poison gas and lists of the dead found in nearly every town square, church and school. A generation of young men lost – and to what purpose?

These memories of the First World War remain with us, even though the last veteran died a few years ago. Every year we still stand silent on the eleventh hour of the eleventh day of the eleventh month, and recall all our war dead. With more recent deaths in places such as Iraq and Afghanistan fresh in our national consciousness, it has become easier to understand again the human sacrifice and sense of loss with every ending of life in combat. War does not seem so remote to us any more. We can therefore get a better grasp of what happened in 1914–1918 than during the recent long years of peace. World War I is relevant again.

Some wars can be described easily. World War II was started by Nazi aggression; about that we have few doubts today. But World War I remains as complex as ever in how it began. Even a century later, debate still rages over who started it and why. We can all see why war broke out in 1939 and why stopping Hitler was necessary. But with 1914, nagging doubts still persist. How did ninety-nine years of peace since Napoleon come to an end, and with such terrible results?

In order to understand this, we need to look at three questions:

1) Why were France and Germany enemies in the first place?
2) What led to war in 1914?
3) Was war inevitable?

We will explore these three questions in the chapters that follow. Historians, like the politicians of an earlier era, still cannot fully agree on who was responsible and why. Yet it is an important discussion even today. We still live with the consequences of the 'Great War' of 1914–1918.

One legacy of this war is the situation in today's Middle East. At the time of writing, fighting is raging in Syria. Once part of the vast Ottoman Empire, Syria was seized by the French as a spoil of war, despite that region being liberated by Australian, British and Arab forces towards the end of World War I. Many of the major problems of the Balkans in the 1990s and the endless violence of the twenty-first-century Middle East stem from the outcome of the battles that we will be examining in this book. There is general agreement that World War II was caused by the inconclusive end to the fighting in 1918. So too, one can argue, was the Cold War. In fact some historians see the various global conflicts as one, either a new Thirty Years' War (1914–1945) or as a 'Short Twentieth Century' of perpetual uncertainty mixed with actual fighting (1914–1989). So the events of 1914 did not just begin four years of war but decades of conflict, certainly up until 1945 and arguably extending to as recently as 1989 and the end of the Cold War.

While the interest in World War I has remained constant, the interpretations of its events have been numerous. History is just like fashion – always changing! The facts remain the same, but how we interpret them changes continually. Someone puts forward a point of view, which everyone believes for a while. Then some revisionists come along and say that the old view was a major misinterpretation, and that a new theory is the one that really represents why something happened. Debate continues and numerous books and articles get written. Finally, many years later, and with much more perspective available as the original events become more distant in time, a final consensus emerges that either takes a middle view between the extremes, or decides that the original view was right in the first place!

Of few events in history is this truer than of the First World War. Reputations come and go. A general is a hero one moment and a lunatic the next. Battles seen at one time as victories become devastating defeats at another. To take one example, Field Marshal Sir Douglas Haig began as a towering hero, following which he was seen as a donkey leading brave lions to their needless deaths. Now, nearly a hundred years after the battles he commanded, he is finally seen as a leader who did his utmost best with the terrible cards he was dealt. Similarly Churchill's terrible errors of judgement at Gallipoli are now seen in the light of the lessons he successfully learnt. Because he saw that the army and the navy should co-ordinate their efforts – as had not happened at Gallipoli – come 1940 he was able to co-ordinate Britain's military effort, save his country from defeat and thereby redeem his reputation.

On what, then, do historians concur? They certainly tend to agree that an old rivalry between France and Germany was a crucial factor in the lead-up to the First World War. In order to understand this we must return to events some decades earlier, and to a war that took place in 1870.

A CONFLICT BETWEEN
TWO COUNTRIES

At the start of 1870, France was an empire, ruled over by
Emperor Napoleon III, the nephew of the great Napoleon
Bonaparte. There was no such country as Germany at this
time, only a number of independent German states. There
was a powerful kingdom in the north of that region, namely
that of Prussia, that stretched from the Dutch border in the
west to the Russian in the east. Alongside Prussia there were
several much smaller kingdoms (such as Bavaria), grand
duchies, principalities and some states of just a few square
miles. These nations had been part of the thousand-year-
old Holy Roman Empire, which lasted from 800–1806,
and which for the last 400 years or so had a ruler from the
House of Habsburg – one of the most important European

royal houses – as its emperor. The attempt by the Austrians to control the future of a potential new German state had been destroyed at a battle in what is now called the Czech Republic, at Sadowa in 1866. The Prussians also coveted being at the heart of a genuinely German nation, in their case one from which Austria would be excluded.

In 1870 Napoleon III fell into a trap laid by the Chancellor (or prime minister equivalent) of Prussia, Otto von Bismarck. This enabled an army under Prussian leadership, but also consisting of troops from the other smaller kingdoms and duchies, such as Saxony and Hesse, to invade French soil. On September 1st 1870 France was completely routed at the Battle of Sedan, a town in northern France. Napoleon III was captured and later deposed and France became a republic, as it has been ever since. The commander of the victorious coalition army was a Prussian general, Helmuth von Moltke, the Elder, who then became one of the most revered soldiers in his country's history.

On January 18th 1871, all the kings, grand dukes and princes whose forces had won at Sedan gathered together for a significant occasion just outside Paris. This gathering only reinforced France's humiliation at the loss of territory. In the Hall of Mirrors in the vast Palace of Versailles, the building constructed to glorify the seventeenth-century French King, Louis XIV, a brand-new country called Germany was created. The Prussian king now became emperor of the new German Empire. It was in fact the Second Reich (the Holy Roman Empire being the First Reich), although few people called it that at the time.

The war that had just happened was called the Franco-Prussian War. But it could equally be called the War that Created Germany. For over a thousand years Germany or its equivalent had been part of larger units, such as the Holy Roman Empire, which included, for example, what is now Austria, Belgium, the Netherlands, the Czech Republic and much of northern Italy in its wider territory. At last, Germany was a country in its own right.

The Germans now added to their new nation areas that had originally been part of the Holy Roman Empire for centuries, but for many years had been an integral part of France. The area we call Alsace, centred on Strasbourg, had been French since as long ago as 1648. Lorraine, centred on the town of Nancy, had swapped sides several times but had been definitively French since the early eighteenth century. Both Alsace and Lorraine were now ceded to the new German Empire.

One key thing must be remembered about this war: Britain played no part. In many other parts of the world, such as the scramble to obtain colonies in Africa, the United Kingdom and France had been rivals for much of the nineteenth century and were not on friendly terms. Now that rivalry was lessening, but still no British soldier would die to help France. And the new little kingdom of Belgium, independent only since 1831 when it broke away from the Netherlands, was neutral, such status having been guaranteed by both Britain and France in a treaty of 1839.

France therefore lost a major war, its emperor and substantial territory to a country that had not existed prior to 1871. This was a total humiliation, and one that the French resolved would never happen again. They drew up a series of plans, the latest of which, by 1914, was called Plan XVII. This made clear that if France and the new German state were ever to be at war, France would immediately invade its former territories – Alsace and Lorraine – in a bid to win them back and also knock Germany out of the fight. But it was not just the French who were making plans.

Having beaten the French easily in 1870, the Germans also drew up plans to ensure that they would be able to do so again. The Prussian General Moltke retired, but one of his successors in charge of the army, Field Marshal Count Alfred von Schlieffen, drew up a master plan on his retirement to ensure that Germany would be able to defeat France easily within forty days. This was critical because as France became friends with the Russian Empire, which lay to the east, the danger existed that the German Empire could find itself at war on two fronts at the same time. We shall look at this in much more detail in the next few chapters, since the infamous Schlieffen Plan was to fail utterly. This was all the more poignant, as the leader of Germany's armies in 1914 was none other than Count Helmuth von Moltke, the Younger, the nephew of the great victor of the 1870s.

In 1914 war did break out, with Germany fighting on two fronts at the same time, against both France and Russia. Everyone, especially the Germans and French, remembered the events of 1870. As the German war machine now went actively into operation, the question was: would France be defeated again?

THE ROAD TO WAR

On the question of who was responsible for the Great War, the victorious Allies in 1919 had no doubts: the Germans started the war and would now pay for it. The Treaty of Versailles, which concluded the main conflict with Germany, had some controversial clauses. Some of the Allies claimed large payments, or reparations, from Germany to pay for the huge losses that Britain and France had suffered as a result of four years of fighting. This was tied to the infamous 'war guilt' clause of the Treaty that specifically accused Germany of starting the conflict and of responsibility for it. Consequently the Germans associated what they believed to be false guilt with the vast payments that they were forced to make to the British and French.

Who caused the outbreak of war in 1914 thus became a political issue rather than a simple matter of historical debate.

Everybody agrees that the trigger that led to war was the murder of Archduke Franz Ferdinand, heir to the Austro-Hungarian throne, by young Bosnian Serb nationalist Gavrilo Princip. The leaders of Austria-Hungary were furious and determined to humiliate the Serbs, whom they deemed responsible for the act, whether indirectly (the government) or directly (the 'Black Hand', rogue elements of Serbian intelligence). Since the path to war clearly began with this shooting and the Austro-Hungarian reaction, questions of 'who started it' might seem a bit odd. Surely, one would think, it was the Austrians who began the conflict? But this is perhaps an overly simplistic way of looking at it. What we should ask instead is this: what was it about the events leading up to World War I that resulted in such a massive and international conflict? Balkan wars had occurred before the Great War without major international involvement. In fact, several had taken place only just prior to 1914, with terrible loss of life but with no Great Power intervention. In 1870 the kingdoms and duchies that were soon to form Germany had invaded France, again without any British action. What was it that made the events in Sarajevo different?

The main suspect has always been the network of alliances that came into being in the late nineteenth and early twentieth centuries. Bismarck, the creator of Germany in 1870, had been careful to ensure that his country did not have enemies on both sides. He had therefore linked Germany to the other two imperial nations, Russia and Austria-Hungary, in the League of the Three Emperors. But in 1890, the young new Emperor of Germany, Kaiser Wilhelm II, who had very different ideas, dismissed Bismarck's caution in international affairs. Germany was still allied to Austria-Hungary, but any sense of friendship with Russia evaporated, so that in 1894 old-fashioned, despotic tsarist Russia signed an alliance with modern, republican, democratic France. Since Poland had been carved up and abolished in the late eighteenth century, this meant that Germany had a hostile power to the west in France and to the east in Russia – what is called 'encirclement', enemies on both sides.

Meanwhile, Britain's alliances were also changing. Historically Britain's enemy had been France. The core state of Germany, the kingdom of Prussia, had been the British ally against French aggression, most notably at the battle of Waterloo in 1815. As recently as 1898 Britain and France had almost gone to war with each other over an oasis in the African desert at Fashoda. But in 1904 the two old enemies had patched up all their differences with the Entente Cordiale. And in 1907 Britain, who had spent much of the nineteenth century hostile to Russia – as during the Crimean War – patched up its differences with the Russians, and reversed centuries of alliances.

All attempts to create a close British-German friendship, however, foundered time and again. As the German economy prospered, Britain was seen not as a potential ally but as a rival. Germany, after its unification in the 1870s, soon became the industrial, economic and scientific powerhouse of Europe. But it was a new country, and increasingly resentful of Britain, which, in addition to its own economic might, was the world's most powerful country with the biggest overseas empire of its age. When the British invented a brand-new kind of battleship, a dreadnought, the Germans decided that they too wanted to have a fleet that matched the Royal Navy. An arms race now ensued, pitting Britain against Germany, just at the very time when Britain and France were friends and not hereditary enemies.

Therefore by 1914 old alliances of ancient vintage had gone and new ones replaced them. But the question arises: how much did these ties in reality bind the countries involved to go to war?

Cutting short volumes of debate and decades of argument, the main thrust of ideas today is that the states that declared war on each other in August 1914 did not fully understand modern warfare. Once an army mobilised, for instance, it was very difficult to get it to stand down again, especially since the comparatively recent invention of railways made transportation much faster than in the past.

And here we need to remember two key things:

1) There had been no major Europe-wide war since Napoleon's defeat at Waterloo in 1815, almost a century earlier: all nineteenth-century wars had been local and had not escalated into wider conflict.

2) European nations completely failed to take on board any of the lessons of the American Civil War, which should have showed clearly what modern weapons could do. 1914 saw new technology combined with pre-Civil War ways of thinking.

Therefore, in allowing the new system of alliances to determine their actions, the European nations really had no idea of what they were letting themselves in for if war broke out. In Britain and Germany, for example, the overwhelming consensus was that war would be over by Christmas. The carnage and millions of deaths were beyond the comprehension and wildest imagination of all those leaders involved in the decision to go to war, and of the men who cheerfully signed up to fight in what everyone thought would be a short and fleeting conflict.

As a result, the escalation of events between Sarajevo at the end of June and the outbreak of hostilities in August, while clear in retrospect to those of us who know what happened next, simply never occurred to the participants *at the time*. In hindsight they are deeply guilty, but they had no idea of what they were unleashing or of the long-term consequences of their actions. It is only through hindsight that we now understand why World War I is so important. Not only were they launching the 'Great War' but everything that stemmed from it: World War II, the Holocaust, the Cold War, Stalin and Mao's purges, the Middle East conflict and all the horrors with which we are still living today.

In essence, one can say that war was caused by the way in which the alliances formed locked countries into their membership. War with one country under such a system automatically led to war with that nation's allies. Russia went to war with Austria-Hungary because the latter had attacked Serbia. As a result Germany went to war with Russia and, as the Russians were allied with France, the French also went to war with Germany.

This, however, is still too simplistic. Although Britain and France had signed agreements with Russia, the British Empire was not obliged to enter the war. The United Kingdom had been neutral when France was defeated in 1870 by what became the newly formed German state. But Britain *had* signed an agreement that guaranteed the neutrality of Belgium in 1839. At that time the fear was of a French invasion of Belgium, as no such state as Germany then existed. When it came to 1914 the French were so anxious not to violate Belgian neutrality that they waited until after the Germans had breached it.

As for other countries, Italy had been allied to Germany and Austria-Hungary since 1882, but in 1915 decided to switch sides and join Britain and France in order to gain territory from Austria. The Ottoman Empire, which ruled over most of today's Middle East and, until 1913, also over much of Europe and North Africa, had been on the same side as Britain and France in the nineteenth century. But the Ottomans' deadliest enemy had for well over a century been Russia – who was now allied to France! So weeks after the war began, the Ottoman Empire switched from its historic allegiance to France and the United Kingdom and entered the war on the side of Germany and Austria-Hungary. So too did the Ottomans' recent former enemy Bulgaria, who had fallen out with Serbia over the spoils of the Ottoman collapse in Europe. Until the war began, therefore, Italy had ignored the alliance system and both Bulgaria and the Ottomans had been outside it.

So, in brief, the powers aligned at the beginning of the Great War were: the Central Powers of Germany and Austria-Hungary, against the Triple Alliance of France, Russia and the British Empire. Later the Ottoman Empire and Bulgaria joined the Central Powers, while Italy (which until 1915 had been theoretically linked to the Central Powers), Japan and the US joined the Allies.

WAS WAR INEVITABLE?

Was war inevitable? Could Britain have kept out of the war as historian Sir Richard Evans suggested on BBC television in 2014? The United Kingdom had not entered into the conflict in 1870. But now, it seems, the situation had changed.

Andrew Adonis, the former Transport Secretary in Gordon Brown's Cabinet, was originally a historian, and he has written about the British Foreign Secretary of 1914, Sir Edward Grey:

Because Sir Edward Grey was such a nice man, historians have followed contemporaries in excusing the fact that he was such a disastrous minister:

arguably the most incompetent Foreign Secretary of all time for his responsibility in taking Britain into the First World War, having failed in July 1914 to do all within his power to stop the conflagration. We cannot know what would have happened had British policy been more effective. Probably it was within the power of Asquith and Grey to have kept Britain out of the war. Possibly they could have prevented it entirely, dissuading Germany from supporting Austria in the chain reaction, which led from Archduke Franz Ferdinand's assassination in Sarajevo on June 28th to the German invasion of Belgium on 4 August. However, since virtually any alternative would have been better than what followed from the calamity of July and August 1914 – namely, a European Thirty Years' War, complete with communism, fascism, genocide, the Holocaust, slavery and the partition and subjugation of Eastern Europe for a further half-century – they deserve little benefit of the doubt.

His views are quoted here at length since it seems that this could, if correct, be a wholly new and vitally needed perspective on World War I. What it argues cogently is that the entire war was unnecessary and could have been avoided, with all that followed from such prevention. So-called 'counterfactual' or 'alternative history', made popular in writing – such as that of Winston Churchill giving Robert E. Lee victory over the Union armies at Gettysburg – loves to ask what would have happened if things had been different. One of the most popular of these counterfactuals is 'what if Princip's bullet had missed in 1914?' Fascinating and fun though that is to ask, it is actually the wrong question. This is because it presumes that the alliances pre-August 1914 locked everyone into inevitable action. Once Sarajevo had happened, this question implies, the Great Powers of Europe were doomed!

But the Adonis thesis, while highly controversial with many historians, is arguably worth full consideration. Even with the Archduke's assassination, war need not have happened. For here one could also agree with the new historical view that *Germany really was guilty after all.* History, as demonstrated in previous chapters, often gets argued over in cycles, and now many would make the case that it was German ambition that triggered war in 1914, far more than the system of alliances.

Again to cut much complex historical narrative and debate short, the Germans actually wanted to have a war, and what happened at Sarajevo gave them the excuse that they wanted. If the Archduke's murder had not occurred, there would have been some other trigger that provided the German Empire with an excuse. In particular they wanted to knock out the Russian Empire before that country's armaments programme really got under way and made a German invasion of Russia more problematic. (This is, of course, exactly what Hitler found when he invaded the USSR in 1941 and duly lost the war as a result.)

For the problem was not the system of alliances per se but the plans that many of the countries had made as to what to do if war began. Here they were locked into unworkable strategies, as the unfolding story of this book will make clear. What sunk Germany was the Schlieffen Plan, about which the next chapter will have much to say. The key thing here is that it involved German troops invading France *through Belgian territory* (and in the original plan through the Netherlands as well). Belgium being neutral, a German attack was a clear breach of that country's internationally guaranteed status, which Britain had sworn seventy-five years ago, in the Treaty of London, to uphold. Britain had ignored France's plight in 1870, but this was another matter. Germany's invasion of Belgium directly threatened the United Kingdom's security, just as possession of the same part of Europe had done during the great wars fought by Marlborough in the early eighteenth century. However, the British leadership – Asquith the Prime Minister and Grey his Foreign Secretary – completely failed to warn Germany in time of the dire consequences of invading Belgium.

The key question, therefore, is not what would have happened if Princip had missed, but this: would Germany still have gone to war if the Germans had known in good time that invading Belgium would mean war with Britain? True, Germany wanted war with Russia, and since France and Russia were allied, that inevitably meant war with France as well. And in turn that meant Germany fighting a two-front war, against France on its west and the Russian Empire on its east. War with the British Empire, however, was another matter – even though the United Kingdom was primarily a naval, not a land-based, military power. So it is a wholly legitimate question to ask. And the 'Adonis thesis' that Germany would *not* have risked war if they had known that Britain was certain to get involved, becomes an important one to ponder, however controversial it might be. In this case the war would never have begun and the world would now be a profoundly different place from the rubble that emerged in 1918.

All this ties in with another new version of history, one that blames Russia for setting the ball rolling and playing unwittingly into the hands of the Germans. Once again the old 'alliances' theory is put under pressure; although Russia mobilised against Austria-Hungary for the latter's threat to and invasion of Serbia, *there was no alliance between Russia and Serbia*. Russia was not going to war on behalf of an ally, but to avenge a humiliation six years earlier in 1908. In the nineteenth century Russia had portrayed itself as the friend of the Slavic peoples of the Balkans. But in 1908, when Austria-Hungary annexed Bosnia, the Russians effectively did nothing to prevent it.

Now in 1914 they were determined to act, and in going to war with Austria-Hungary they were making up for their failures six years earlier.

Thus the original sequence of events June to August 1914:

a) Princip assassinates the Archduke Franz Ferdinand.

b) The enraged Austrians give an impossible ultimatum to the Serbs, which in turn brings Russia into the war.

c) Because Russia and Austria-Hungary are at war, Germany sides with their ally, and thus goes to war with Russia and France.

d) By invading France via Belgium, the Germans bring Britain into the war as well.

However, this traditional account leaves out three vital things:

1) The Germans wanted a pre-emptive knockout war with Russia and thus also with that country's French ally.

2) The British failed adequately to make clear to

Germany the dire consequences of war through Belgium.

3) Russia need not have gone to war to help Serbia but did so out of choice rather than necessity.

The original account blames the hotheads in Vienna, determined to crush Serbia whatever the consequences. This version clearly makes Austria-Hungary the creator of World War I, since it was their invasion of Serbia that brought in Russia and thus Germany and France as well. According to this interpretation, therefore, Germany is innocent – and both Hitler and the millions of Germans who supported him were right to say that the Allies were unfair in blaming Germany for starting the war and insisting on reparation payments in the Treaty of Versailles.

But the archives now show that Germany wanted an excuse for war, and that Russian militarism played into their hands by bringing the Russian Empire into the war against Germany's ally Austria-Hungary. So even if Russian aggression lit the actual fuse, it is Germany that is truly to blame, because there was no way in which an empire as ramshackle and multi-ethnic as that of Austria-Hungary could have fought the Russians on its own. They had to have German support, and this they received, thereby giving the Germans the excuse for war with Russia that so many wanted.

So this is where some recent thinking on Britain and its role enters in. Germany would not have given the Austrians permission to attack Serbia if the Germans had known that this in turn would lead inevitably to war with both Britain and its entire empire. (Remember in those days war with Britain meant war against Canada, Australia and New Zealand as well, not to mention India.)

What, then, if the British had made abundantly clear to the Germans from the outset that war with France would mean war with Britain as well? Might this have happened?

a) Germany tells Austria-Hungary not to invade Serbia and to accept the Serb compliance with the bulk of the Austrian ultimatum.

b) Austria-Hungary accepts Serbia's apologies.

c) Russia therefore has no excuse to attack Austria-Hungary.

d) Germany therefore realises that the price for attacking Russia is too high – that of British involvement against them.

e) Germany therefore stays at peace and leaves France and Russia alone.

f) World War I does not happen and the German excuse to invade Russia finds no outlet.

g) Hitler dies as an obscure artist in Munich. Stalin is arrested by the democratically elected Russian government and dies in obscurity in prison while Lenin dies a disappointed exile in Switzerland.

h) The Ottoman Empire survives in the Middle East, with the small Jewish minority in Palestine living peacefully with its mainly Christian Arab neighbours.

i) Theodore Herzl dies in Britain, one of the 50 million Jewish people living happily in Europe with their Gentile neighbours. Germany's most distinguished scientist Albert Einstein is elected President of Germany.

How very different the rest of the twentieth century would have been.

It is of course equally possible that a German-launched war would have happened within a few years nonetheless. But it would have been in very different circumstances. The Austro-Hungarian Empire might well have still collapsed, but through internal civil war, with the Hungarians resisting the rule of the new Emperor Karl.

What all this shows is that World War I was never inevitable, but arose from conscious choices, most notably the deliberate sins of commission by Germany and those of omission by Britain, with Russian decisions also playing a pivotal role. And today, even one hundred years later, we still live with the consequences.

In conclusion, one other thought is worth pondering. As historian Max Hastings argues in his book *Catastrophe* on 1914, Germany, while no Third Reich, was nonetheless an aggressive and militaristic nation. Once war actually began, in contrast to my counterfactual peace above, it was worth fighting the German Empire. Hastings shows that victory for the Kaiser in such a conflict would have created a Europe in which democratic values would have struggled to prevail. Britain would have been horribly isolated and the USA would have remained cut off from Europe, a despotic Old World that most Americans had fled.

So, better that the war had never happened, but once it did, better that Britain and eventually the USA became involved, for the sake of the values for which they stood.

PART ONE

WAR ON MANY FRONTS

THE BATTLE OF THE FRONTIERS

August 2nd–26th 1914

In his famous five-volume work *The World Crisis*, Winston Churchill wrote presciently on the opening of the conflict: 'The War was decided in the first twenty days of fighting, and all that happened afterwards consisted in battles which, however formidable and devastating, were but desperate and vain appeals against the decision of Fate.'

In terms of a description of what was to happen on the front lines between the German and Allied positions after the Battle of the Frontiers was over, this account cannot be bettered. As we shall see, the nations of Western Europe (and after 1917 their American associate) did not manage to break out of a terrible stalemate for four bloodstained years, in which hundreds of thousands of courageous men died to gain what was often no more than just a few yards of soil.

But what determined where those trenches would be situated, strung out as they were from the Atlantic Ocean to the Swiss border, across southern Belgium and northern France? And why, unlike in 1870 and a more famous German victory in 1940, did the French manage to defy fate and hold out against their invaders? The next few chapters will explain the reasons why.

Churchill was almost right in ascribing the outcome to a mere twenty days. Most historians reckon that the 'Battle for the Frontiers' lasted from August 2nd to August 26th, just four days longer. Churchill was right, as we shall see, to ascribe the outcome of the war to the very earliest engagements between the two enemies, the Allies (the United Kingdom, France and Russia) and the Central Powers (Germany, Austria-Hungary and soon thereafter the Ottoman Empire).

Churchill's view would in many ways seem obvious. Max Hastings, one of the doyens of British military history, agrees in his book *Catastrophe: Europe Goes to War in 1914* with the wisdom of following a Churchillian understanding of events. Some academic historians have found this approach slightly simplistic, and there are of course always tiny exceptions to every generalisation if one wants a highly nuanced perspective. But the simplest explanation in a glance at the events of August 1914 would seem to coincide with what one can call the Churchill/

Hastings idea: that Germany tried to invade and conquer France in rapid time, and in failing to accomplish that goal assured their own eventual defeat four years later.

Plans can be realistic. But they can also be fantasy if all the possible contingencies are not taken into account.

There is an excellent case for saying that the carefully laid down and minutely prescribed Schlieffen Plan, in which the Germans were placing total faith, was in truth based on fantasy, not reality. For all depended upon three factors:

1) an extraordinarily tight timetable,

2) that nothing would happen that was not already in the plan itself and, above all,

3) that the German army would manage to vanquish its foes.

One small delay, unexpected event or successful piece of French resistance and the whole edifice of Schlieffen was in danger of falling down like a pack of cards.

We shall be looking at the outcome of the Schlieffen Plan in detail as the next few chapters of this book unfold. But let us go back to the beginning, when the Germans still had belief and hope, and the war that they had long anticipated now became a reality.

On August 3rd and 4th the German invasion of Belgium began. Belgian neutrality had been strictly observed in 1870 and now it was ignored. And because of that decision, Britain did what it had not done in 1870 and joined in the war, because of the Treaty of 1839 that guaranteed Belgium's inviolability. On August 2nd the Grand Duchy of Luxembourg had also been invaded. This tiny country was also theoretically neutral, under the rule of its Grand Duchess. But it fell, along with its great fortress, and entered German hands.

Whether Britain would perhaps have gone to war in 1914 just to protect France is a moot point, one much discussed by historians and strategists ever since. But most people agreed that Belgium was sacrosanct, and so the United Kingdom and thus (in those days) its Empire as well declared war on Germany.

Now a key part of Schlieffen had become unstuck, since no allowance for Britain entering the war had been made. While the British Expeditionary Force, Britain's own troops were, as we shall see later, tiny compared to the French and German behemoths, even the BEF's very existence did tip the scales in France's favour in a way for which Schlieffen had not planned. Within a few days, many other declarations of war had taken place, one of these being that of Japan against the Central Powers, a factor that considerably increased the scope of what had been simply a European war. As well as ignoring the likely

British action, Schlieffen did not allow for anything like the Belgian degree of resistance that now ensued. This was still the honeymoon period of the war, with millions of troops going into battle all expecting that the war would be over by Christmas. Reading what people wrote or expressed back in the summer of 1914 is extraordinary. The degree of optimism, which was mutually contradictory as it was held as absolute truth by each side, was so soon to be crushed. The millions cheering their country's forces were in the ultimate fool's paradise. This makes 1914 utterly different from 1939, when everyone knew all too well what might be coming next.

Belgium had an army that was not much bigger than the size of the British Expeditionary Force now embarking from England. But the country possessed some of the most powerful forts in the world, in particular that protecting the city of Liège. Today, with air power a major component of any war, faith in fortifications seems somewhat quaint. In those days, however, it was a vital part of a nation's protection, from Belgium to Austria-Hungary over to Russia. In addition, Liège had some outer forts, so a great deal would need to be captured to render the entire system inoperable.

The original Schlieffen Plan had required Germany to breach Dutch as well as Belgian neutrality. Wiser counsels had prevailed and that idea within the Plan had been sensibly dropped. But the issue remained – should the invading German armies wheel past Liège and opt to take the fortress later once they were well on their victorious way to Paris, or should the fortress and its satellites be seized first?

On August 5th German troops began the bombardment of Liège. General Gérard Leman decided to hold the fortress until the last, and so a longer siege than had been anticipated now began. Fortunately for the Germans, one of their greatest commanders now came to the rescue of the invaders. This was General Erich Ludendorff, an expert in logistics and in possible alternative ways of winning a war. He decided to employ Zeppelins, the huge airships that had been invented in Germany not long before. The fortress was not seriously damaged but many civilians died in the air raid, the first of many who would be slaughtered by a German army decreasingly concerned with human rights.

By August 7th the main citadel had been breached, but several of the smaller forts were still holding out zealously. Ludendorff now decided to utilise the 'Big Bertha', a massive gun manufactured by the German armaments firm Krupp, one that was to remain notorious over the years ahead. And one interesting codicil: the 'Big' of 'Big Bertha' was a reference not to the physical size of Bertha Krupp, after whom the guns were said to be named, but to that of the artillery pieces themselves! On August 12th the Big Berthas began to fire, with powerful shells specially designed to break through substances such as concrete. This worked where all else had failed. On August 16th even the forts were compelled to surrender. Since the poor Belgian commander General Leman had been knocked out, he was truthfully able to say that he had not himself agreed to give in to the German assault.

Vital days had now been lost, but the French were determined still, against all evidence to the contrary, to stick to their Plan XVII and launch a major offensive against the Germans in Alsace and Lorraine. Meanwhile British troops had landed, as described later in the chapter on the Battle of Mons. This meant that although the Schlieffen Plan had gone awry, no major army existed to prevent the Germans from their planned assault, now into France itself.

The Germans were, while in occupation of most of Belgium, terrified of a resistance movement. Therefore they decided on draconian measures to ensure that the Belgian people did not manage to carry out acts of sabotage or other forms of resistance. Countless atrocities now took place. In the town of Dinant, for example, no fewer than 612 civilians were massacred. Shockingly, when 384 similarly innocent people were butchered, the atrocity happened in broad daylight in the town square.

In Louvain, then as now one of the great intellectual centres of Europe, far worse horrors were perpetrated by an increasingly jumpy and paranoid German occupying army. One of the world's finest libraries was in this city and was now burnt to the ground, with no fewer than 230,000 rare and irreplaceable books being destroyed. Some 209 civilians were simply massacred and tens of thousands of citizens forced to evacuate the area.

This created huge international outrage against Germany, critically including large waves of disgust in the still neutral United States. While leading German intellectuals such as the scientist Max Planck were embarrassed by their fellow countrymen, the path to the even greater atrocities of the Holocaust and the Russian Front of future years had now been taken. The Allies had a major propaganda coup and the war was still only a few days old.

So far as the French were concerned, however, the main war was still hundreds of miles away in Alsace-Lorraine! Much hard fighting took place there, since the German armies now under attack did not wish to remain inactive. Soon, French troops that were supposed to be liberating Alsace-Lorraine found themselves in ignominious retreat.

The French commander actually near the real fighting on the Belgian border, General Charles Lanrezac, was in a terrible position. He knew that the Germans were on the attack nearby. At the same time he was aware that official French policy was ignoring the realities altogether and concentrating its main armies miles away from where they were truly needed. Thankfully for him, the overall French commander, General Joseph Joffre, finally realised by August 15th that things were not as they ought to be. So he allowed Lanrezac's army to go north to Namur, nearer the action.

On August 21st the French and Germans finally met, and fought what is called the Battle of the Sambre. This has rightly been nicknamed a 'bloody slugfest'. The French were acting defensively, awaiting the Germans, and the latter were ready for battle. So while the British were fighting their hardest not far away at Mons, General Lanrezac decided on August 24th simply to retreat.

By this time both the Allies were in retreat, fleeing towards Paris and away from the Germans, the British having done their best at Mons and Le Cateau. France's disastrous Plan XVII had cost them at least 300,000 casualties. Joffre realised too late that a plan to which he himself had given so much credence was an utter failure. He told the French government that their armed forces had been 'condemned to a defensive attitude'.

But as we shall soon discover, Joffre's ability to change plans saved France, whereas rigid German adherence to the last letter of the Schlieffen Plan would now have the opposite effect. The Allies had been brutally mauled, but all was not yet lost.

THE BATTLE OF MONS

August 23rd 1914

The Battle of Mons, on the Belgian side of the border with France, was the first engagement of the new British Expeditionary Force and thus, for them, of the war. It was their contribution to the wider Battle of the Frontiers against the Germans.

The overall commander was Sir John French, who had been Chief of the Imperial General Staff until resigning in disputed circumstances over a failed mutiny in Ireland earlier that year. Under him were two corps commanders, Sir Horace Smith-Dorrien, now faded from memory, and Sir Douglas Haig. The latter was to go on to succeed French as the BEF's overall commander and become one of the most famous and controversial generals in British history.

The BEF who fought at Mons were all regular soldiers. Many of these had signed up for several years' worth of military service, with the long-terms having fought in colonial wars, such as the Boer War in South Africa. Just before the conflict, they had, so it was said at the time, been nicknamed 'contemptible' by the German Kaiser, Wilhelm II. They gave themselves the proud moniker of the 'Old Contemptibles' as a result.

The BEF were around 80,000 strong – large for a British army but minuscule in comparison with the vast conscript forces of Germany and France. With their professionalism – not to mention their very accurate Enfield rifles – they were supposed to be a real match for the Germans. So accurately did the soldiers shoot and with such rapidity that their opponents thought mistakenly that the British had machine guns. However, as many writers have now revealed, the BEF was against a massively bigger foe than they expected: the German 1st Army under General Alexander von Kluck.

As previous chapters have illustrated, French strategy, in particular Plan XVII, presupposed a strike into Alsace-Lorraine, the territories stolen by Germany from France in 1870. French military doctrine was aggressive rather than defensive, so their armies were poised for attacking German soil rather than defending the frontiers against a German invasion.

This suited the Germans greatly, since they planned

to attack France through *Belgian* territory with a massive right-hook advance aimed to arrive at the right of the French capital, Paris, while the other army would invade from the left.

This was in essence the Schlieffen Plan, the German war plan invented at the turn of the century by their Army Chief of Staff General Count Alfred von Schlieffen. His original draft, in fact, had the Germans also transgressing Dutch territory around Maastricht. In view of what now happened it was just as well for Germany that they did not drag the Netherlands into the war as well.

Britain, as we saw in the introduction, was only at war because of the German violation of Belgian neutrality. This was because to enter the conflict for an attack purely on France would not necessarily have enjoyed the consensus in the country and in the government itself that the assault on Belgium provided.

Consequently Britain had not, despite several years of helpful staff talks between the British and French armies, prepared as fully as might have been useful when war actually began. Inevitably, the professional soldiers and senior commanders, while possessing decades of experience, had none whatsoever against a modern and well-equipped force such as the Germans they now faced. Kitchener, the great British field marshal, and former commander-in-chief in both Egypt and in India, was now Secretary of State for War. While he was aware of the deficiencies, the same accusation could be made against him. Fighting the Boers was one thing, even with a Lee–Enfield rifle, but opposing the juggernaut that was the German 1st Army was quite another matter.

The Battle of Mons was therefore first blood for the British. The fact that they survived to escape, and to retreat many miles almost to the French capital, is tribute in and of itself. Many would regard it as a victory, because although they were compelled to retreat from their entrenched positions, they were able to do so in good order and in a position to fight another day. This they were compelled to do on August 26th at the Battle of Le Cateau. The German advance still continued, but had been slowed by British resistance. Indeed, as events would later turn out, that was to be just as well for the survival of France. In the light of later casualties, such as at Ypres or at the Somme, the dead and injured total for the BEF of just over 1,200 was wonderfully low. But for the next two weeks, as the whole BEF retreated before the powerful right hook of the German advance, it looked as if the Allies could have lost the war before it had hardly begun. But as we shall see when looking at the Siege of Liège and the victorious Battle of the Marne, the British-French-Belgian cause was not over yet.

The British may have been required to retreat, but the fact that they were there at all shows that the Schlieffen Plan had already gone wrong. It had not allowed for British involvement in the war. In fact, its attack through neutral Belgium had precipitated British entry. In comparison to the conscript armies of France and Germany, 80,000 soldiers might not be much, but their existence and presence alongside the French was in itself a major delay to the minutely choreographed German plans. The BEF grew to hundreds of thousands as the war progressed and the importance of this diversion from the plan increased commensurately.

The question of the Schlieffen Plan will be explored in later chapters. However, before we look at the Battle of the Marne and the Allied success in halting the Germans, there is a fascinating new 'what if?' to add to the alternative history of World War I.

The main reason for 'counterfactual history', to use the official phrase, is to show that nothing that happened in history was ever inevitable. As we saw in the introduction, counterfactuals mainly consider large-scale events along the lines of 'what if Franz Ferdinand had not been killed at Sarajevo?' In the case of 1914, the British writer and former soldier Allan Mallinson has raised the fascinating notion of 'what if Kitchener and Haig's advice had been taken on where to place the BEF?'

Alongside this, he also notes a genuine Churchill memorandum of 1911, suggesting that any such force could or should have been much bigger – so what if

Churchill's retrospectively wise advice had been taken? Thirdly, he speculates, suppose the French, when realising that the Italians were going to stay neutral, had decided to move the key divisions away from the Italian frontier and up to the border with Belgium? Since Italy was to switch sides in favour of the Allies in 1915, this is a legitimate question to ponder.

There is no reason why the BEF could not have been 300,000 strong instead of just 80,000, if it had been sent just a few weeks later than was actually the case. In this alternative scenario, the French forces against which the Germans crashed with such force would have been much stronger. And if Haig and Kitchener had prevailed in the discussions, a much larger BEF of 300,000 troops would have been ready in Amiens – not up near the border at Mons – ready and waiting.

In Mallinson's cheerful scenario, so badly would the German invasion have been derailed – far more than it was in reality – that surrender or a negotiated peace in 1915 might have been a viable outcome. In which case there would have been no trenches, no Battle of the Somme, millions would have lived rather than being killed, there would have been no Russian Revolution in 1917 and ultimately no Hitler either.

This is all taking us a long way from the Battle of Mons, and those battles that followed immediately thereafter, especially the Allied fightback in the Battle of the Marne.

It is perhaps rather optimistic! But more realistically Mallinson does argue that it might have been possible, had things been planned differently, for the Allies to have held on to far more of Belgium than in fact turned out to be the case. In this perhaps more viable alternative, there would, for example, have been far more ports to which to bring supplies and more Allied-held territory to bring the front closer to the German border.

Victory in 1915 might not have happened, and there would still have been trenches and carnage. But the war could *possibly* have ended sooner than it did. There might still have been a Somme, but perhaps not a Passchendaele.

Back now to the actual events of 1914. If the Germans stuck to their plans, the French did not. As soon as Joffre realised where the real enemy assault was coming from, he was able in effect to scrap Plan XVII, give up the invasion of Alsace and Lorraine, and send his armies to halt the German juggernaut. There would not be another 1870.

THE BATTLE OF TANNENBERG

August 26th–30th 1914

Few battles have had novels written about them by Nobel Prize winners. *August 1914*, by Alexandr Solzhenitsyn, is an exception. This novel is based upon the so-called 'Battle of Tannenberg' between the Russians and Germans. Tannenberg is in fact a completely misleading name for what was, some argue, not even an important battle. But it is one whose iconic status is considerable, which is why so much attention has been paid to it ever since. Furthermore, the battles on the Eastern Front, between the German and Russian armies, while little known in the West, did have a major impact on their far more famous equivalents in Flanders and northern France. Not only that, but the death count was every bit as high in Central/Eastern Europe as in Western. While we in

Britain or the USA might have forgotten epic encounters such as Tannenberg or its follow-up, the even less familiar Battle of the Masurian Lakes, Germans and Russians have not, with consequences that still live with us in the twenty-first century.

Tannenberg in 1914 was, strictly speaking, the Battle of Allenstein, a town in German-ruled East Prussia. But in 1410 the great Crusader-founded Order, the Teutonic Knights, were wiped out by a brave Polish army, at Tannenberg, a shame that the Germans – the 'Teutonic' race – never forgot. To the Germans the symbolism of Tannenberg was the same even though the Poles were not Russians and vice versa. (Just to make life interesting, *that* battle really happened at a place called Grünwald, so even to name that encounter as Tannenberg is also misleading.) In 1914 there was no Poland, that poor nation having been carved up in the late eighteenth century by the Austrian and Russian Empires and by the German state, the Kingdom of Prussia. However, Poles and Russians are both Slavs, so melded in the minds of their German opponents.

The Russians had begun war well. Within the first month, two of their armies were on German soil, in what was then East Prussia. However, the two key commanders, General Alexander Samsonov and General Paul von Rennenkampf (of ethnic German Baltic origin but a Russian soldier) disliked one another and failed utterly to co-ordinate their plans. In addition, since radio communication was complex the Russians sent messages *en clair*, which meant that they could all be intercepted and read easily by the Germans, who were able to enter combat with full knowledge of what their opponents were planning. The Russians' eventual goal was the capture of the famous East Prussian town of Königsberg, the original heartland of the former German rulers of the area, the Teutonic Knights.

As the German high command was horrified that Russian soldiers were on Prussian soil, they replaced their own existing commanders with new generals. One was the semi-retired General Paul von Hindenburg and the other, his chief of staff, General Erich Ludendorff. Both these names would become historic, with Hindenburg ending up as President of Germany after the war (and Hitler's predecessor in this post) and Ludendorff as a failed forerunner of Nazi ideology. Their days of fame were now about to begin, as Samsonov's army walked straight into the trap that the Germans had prepared for them.

Before skirmishes began – remember, Hindenburg knew exactly what Samsonov was planning – two new German divisions arrived from France to help their colleagues against the Russians. Strategically this was not necessary as Hindenburg and Ludendorff had the matter well in hand. But it was great news for the British and French facing the German invaders in Flanders and northern France. As that invasion only narrowly failed, it could be that the transfer of troops away from the Western Front to the East made the crucial difference.

Initial skirmishes took place between the various German and Russian divisions from August 23rd, with the main battle itself, between the German 8th Army and the Russian 2nd Army, taking place between August 26th and 30th. The Russians were utterly routed. So humiliated was Samsonov that he committed suicide rather than return to his home country in shame. Some 78,000 Russians were killed or wounded, around 92,000 captured and some 10,000 managed to escape. German casualties were 20,000 killed or wounded, which was high but nowhere near as grave as the Russian losses.

Many historians have argued that the First Battle of the Masurian Lakes (September 7th–14th) was technically more important than Tannenberg, as it enabled the Germans to expel Rennenkampf's 1st Army from Prussian soil. The Russians were to do very well against the other Central Power, Austria-Hungary, as we shall see, but they never again bested the Germans in battle. By 1917, thanks to the Bolshevik Revolution in November that year, a non-tsarist Russia was out of the war altogether.

But Tannenberg was iconic all the same, and enabled the Germans to feel that they had enjoyed a major victory, especially when their forces in Western Europe had been ground to a halt by the British, French and Belgians. Hindenburg and Ludendorff were later to end the war in the West. Because of their heroic status at Tannenberg, they were deemed unsackable by the High Command in a way that other generals, who lacked their victorious aura, were not. Since Ludendorff's strategy, especially in 1918, was to turn out disastrously, this was perhaps just as well for Britain and France.

In the 1920s and 1930s the Germans, while remembering their loss of the war to the Western Allies, never forgot that *on the Eastern Front Germany won the war*, and that it was only defeat in the West that caused them to surrender. Hitler certainly never forgot it. In 1941 he was to launch '*Barbarossa*', the Nazi invasion of the USSR, perhaps the biggest such attack in history. This invasion left tens of millions of Germans and Russians dead. Nor did the Russians forget it, with the creation of the Soviet bloc around the USSR in 1945 and decades of Communist domination of Central and Eastern Europe until 1989. Today much of former German East Prussia remains part of the Russian Federation, even long after the Cold War.

THE BATTLES OF CER MOUNTAIN AND KOLUBARA

August–December 1914

The Austro-Hungarian Empire had gone to war in 1914 in order to punish Serbia. They soon realised that their main enemy would be the Russian Empire, who attacked the Austro-Hungarian province of Galicia (most of whose inhabitants were Polish or Ukrainian). But while their concentration therefore had to be on that front, nonetheless the original war aim of occupying and crushing Serbia had to proceed.

The two battles described here are almost totally unknown in the West, although they live in Serb folklore to this day. But they show also that the great Austro-Hungarian Empire was militarily disastrous, even from the outset of the war. The Empire's forces were supposedly some of the finest and best equipped in Europe. But this was swiftly revealed as an illusion, even against tiny Serbia, many of whose soldiers did not even own shoes. The last war in which the Austrians had fought was in 1866, and that too had been a major defeat.

The Serbs, however, had excellent and recent battle experience, being on the victorious side of the two Balkan Wars of 1912–1913. They had no fewer than 400,000 soldiers ready to fight, whatever their level of equipment. In Field Marshal Radomir Putnik they had a commander of genuine skill, as opposed to the Austro-Hungarian General Oskar Potiorek, a rival for power of the overall imperial commander, Field Marshal Count Conrad von Hötzendorf.

The Austro-Hungarian army began its attack on August 12th 1914. Had the Serbs kept to their original battle plan, they would have walked straight into a trap. But Putnik's reconnaissance forces found the enemy and he was able to turn his entire army ninety degrees and launch a successful night attack on the invaders at the Battle of Cer Mountain. By August 24th the invaders had successfully been expelled from Serb soil. By the beginning of September, Serb forces were able to invade Bosnia and come within range of Sarajevo itself.

This proved to be as far as they could reach. The Austrians counter-attacked and by November the Serb capital, Belgrade, had fallen to them. Austro-Hungarian might had apparently prevailed after all. Putnik, however, decided to strike back, fully supported by Serbia's King Peter, who told his forces that while they could flee if they wanted to, he would stay to fight. The Battle of Kolubara, December 3rd–15th, justified their persistence. The Serbs launched a new attack, and were completely successful. Belgrade was recaptured and once more the invaders were expelled from Serbian soil.

There are major disagreements on the numbers of casualties. If one takes historian David Stevenson's figures as the best guide, Potiorek's forces lost 28,000 dead, 120,000 wounded and over 76,000 as prisoners. The Serbs lost 22,000 dead, 92,000 wounded and 19,000 as prisoners – as Serbia was far smaller, this makes their losses comparatively far higher.

But the gallant Serbs had won! Huge amounts of aid from other parts of Europe now poured in to help them, a David against the Austrian Goliath. Tragically for Serbia, though, this was not the end of the story, for in the autumn of 1915 the Germans came to the aid of their ally, and the Serbs were swiftly overrun and forced into exile.

But the fact that the might of the Austro-Hungarian Empire could not, *on its own*, defeat even tiny Serbia spoke volumes. The Empire had started the war but it could not carry it through without overwhelming German help. And with the failure of the German army to crush France, Austria-Hungary's only effective ally was heavily preoccupied elsewhere. The outlook for Emperor Franz Joseph and his forces was grim. These two battles can serve as permanent reminders that military strength by itself can be meaningless and that the plight of the Central Powers, as Austria-Hungary, Germany, Bulgaria and Turkey came to be known, was dire.

THE BATTLES OF THE CARPATHIANS

August 1914–March 1915

The Carpathian Mountains, one of Europe's grandest ranges, are sadly little known in Western Europe and the wider world. Yet they are the region from which, for example, millions of Americans descend, their ancestors having emigrated from there to the USA in the nineteenth and early twentieth centuries, when most of it was still ruled by the theoretically mighty Austro-Hungarian Empire.

In the south the Austro-Hungarian Empire was hostile to the new Serb state, especially after a coup in 1903 had installed a dynasty that the Habsburg emperors did not trust. In the north their foe was the vast Russian Empire, with its enormous army. More importantly, Russia had endless supplies of replacements in its huge population, however many hundreds of thousands would die on the Russian vs. Austro-Hungarian battle front.

Replacement is one of the little thought-of but vital facets of war, especially if the conflict lasts for more than just a few months. Russia's population was so gigantic that they could replace countless forces lost in battle, a key factor that Hitler was to forget, to his grave disadvantage, in 1941–1945. Whole Russian armies could be destroyed, but there would always be fresh soldiers of military age to replace those who had been killed or captured.

Replacement was a major concern for both Austria-Hungary and Germany. Although their populations were large, their numbers were yet much smaller than those of Russia. As we shall see when considering the Allied victory in 1918, the sheer scale of the new American arrivals – hundreds of thousands of troops a month coming across from the USA – was one of the key tipping points in the German defeat.

With Austria-Hungary there was another factor – the political and patriotic reliability of their army. Ethnic Germans and Hungarians could have their loyalty taken for granted. Some of those regiments now sent into battle against the Russians were soldiers of impeccable German origin with ancient loyalties to the ruling Habsburg dynasty. But such was not equally the case for thousands of other conscripts, for example those of Slavic origin, obliged to fight for an emperor of a different race against an army consisting of Russians, their fellow Slavs.

In practice Austrian or Hungarian rule (depending upon which side of the dividing line you lived) was often tolerated but not loved. Poles, for example, largely preferred being ruled by Austrians to being subjects of the Russian Tsar. But left to their own choice many of them would have wished to restore the once mighty Poland back to its pre-eighteenth-century status as an independent kingdom. Other subject peoples, such as the Czechs and Slovaks, could not be relied upon for loyalty to the Habsburg rulers.

Yet it was members of all these many and varied ethnic groups that made up the large numbers of the Austro-Hungarian Army. In the 1860s the various ethnic Poles, Czechs and Hungarians had been asked to fight the Prussians, and were defeated ignominiously. Now Prussia, the former enemy, was the core constituent of the new German state, and thus no longer the Empire's enemy but their ally. So not only was there the natural problem of replacement of those killed, but also one of the prospect of mass desertions, of say Slovaks who would far rather fight *with* the Russians than against them. Soon not even the loyalty of the Poles could be guaranteed.

To begin with, the war actually went well for Conrad, the Austro-Hungarian army's chief of staff, and the troops under his command. The Austro-Hungarian armies won two key battles against the invading Russian forces in the summer of 1914, at Kraśnik and Komarów.

But if some British and French generals were to prove not exactly up to speed in command of modern warfare, their lack of ability pales into insignificance in comparison with the incompetence and frequent over-optimism of the Austrian leadership. No sooner had they won than they found themselves opposite General Aleksei Brusilov, the greatest Russian commander of the war and probably one of the best on either side throughout.

In September 1914, the Russians captured the great fortress of Lemberg, supposedly the kind of fortification that was built to withstand such sieges. The Austrians were therefore forced to withdraw on September 11th. They lost 400,000 men out of 1.8 million mobilised, including 300,000 as prisoners. As historian Correlli Barnett writes, the Russians 'inflicted a wound on the morale of [the] . . . multiracial army from which it would never really recover'. Worse still, according to John Keegan, 40,000 of the losses were the elite ethnic German Tyrolean regiments. This lost Austria 'its best and bravest elements, never to be replaced'.

Battles now raged around various parts of Central Europe, including intense fighting for Warsaw, which in those days was a Russian town. The Austro-Hungarian army now had its sole unaided victory of the war, at Limanowa-Łapanów. As a result, they no longer had to fear a Russian attack that, if not hindered, might have reached as far as the Hungarian capital, Budapest.

But here the differences between the two enemies now became stark. By early 1915 the Russian army had been reduced from around three and a half million to around two million. However, they had *ten million* reserves, young men of military age with the potential to be called up to fight. By contrast, the Austro-Hungarian army, which was fighting against Serbia as well as Russia, had lost 1.28 million out of a starting total of just over three million. Their replacement maximum has been estimated at less than two million, overwhelmingly smaller than the Russian potential. Not only that, but with the best ethnic German troops gone, the Austro-Hungarian leadership had to rely on extremely unreliable minority groups to keep fighting. Their loyalty was far from guaranteed.

Then, on March 22nd, the Russians captured the great Carpathian fortress of Przemyśl, one of the key strongholds of the defence system of the Austro-Hungarian Empire. They promptly tried to demolish it, and seized 2,500 officers and 117,000 other men as prisoners. By the end of that month the Habsburg Empire had lost 800,000 in the first quarter of 1915 alone, on top of the already disastrous 1914 losses. From now on they would have to depend completely upon their German ally to keep them in the war at all.

THE BATTLE OF THE MARNE

September 6th–12th 1914

The fight to save France after the German assault via the Schlieffen Plan has been called the 'miracle on the Marne'. It was the one time out of their three confrontations when the French beat the German invaders, unlike in both 1870 and 1940.

The historical consensus has been that the German General Moltke now proceeded to lose the plot and 'in so doing, threw away victory in the Great War'. In particular, he is alleged to have deviated from the Schlieffen Plan in such a way that Germany lost the key advantage, as we saw at the Battle of Mons.

This view, however, presumes rather a lot. The Plan had already been seriously delayed by the bravery of the

Belgians and the siege of Liège. Although the BEF was not an army on the German or French scale, its presence did make a key difference. Finally, the supply routes for the invaders were now getting exceptionally long. A running theme throughout the war was that armies that got too far ahead of the ability to support them logistically would always get into trouble, and the Germans in 1914 were no exception.

Some of the changes of manoeuvre we are about to see can get remarkably complex. But the key question is surely: did slight deviations from Schlieffen's sacred text *actually* make any difference? Or was it the case that, with the delay in reaching their destination, the Germans had in effect blown the chance of victory already? And how crucial was the fact that the French under Joffre now got their act together? In considering the autumn of 1914 we almost certainly underestimate France's military leadership.

French politicians were another matter. Many of them thought that 1870 had come again and they made preparations to flee the capital. Germany had conquered huge swathes of northern France, Plan XVII had proved a disaster and now the Germans were on the edge of Paris.

Thankfully the new Military Governor of Paris, General Joseph-Simon Gallieni, was made of sterner stuff. He refused to regard Paris as a defenceless object, and demanded enough troops to ring the capital effectively. While Joffre decided to keep as many soldiers as possible, Gallieni started to prepare Paris to be ready to fight. Famously, even the taxis of the capital were pressed into service to transport men and material, though sadly for the legend this action was not to be as instrumental in saving the capital as the myth would have us believe.

Now the Parisians were also helped by the interconnected nature of war. So overconfident had the Germans become that they felt that they could spare two whole divisions to be transferred to the Eastern Front. Since Hindenburg was winning well without such help, this gesture was unnecessary. But for the capture of Paris, sending away forces that could have made a critical difference was a foolish move.

Meanwhile the British were showing their mettle. At the Battle of Le Cateau on August 25th–27th, they were, astonishingly, able to delay the onward march of the German forces under General Alexander von Kluck. Then it was the French turn to show that they too could win against the invaders. At Guise they were able to halt the other German army, under General Karl von Bülow.

British and French success against their German foes was not part of the Schlieffen Plan. In fact the Plan seemed not to allow for any defeat at all, so one could argue that it was now *already* in terminal trouble. This is an important point. The traditional view has been that

Bülow, in difficulties because of his losses to the French at Guise, now threw away the Schlieffen Plan by requesting help from his German co-commander Kluck. Under Schlieffen, Kluck was supposed to wheel around Paris and take the city. But now there was a deviation from the sacred writ. As one American writer has commented, what Kluck now did 'would alter the course of the next four years'.

All this had been exacerbated by Moltke's decision to allow his key army commanders to use their own initiative when necessary, rather than follow the Plan rigidly under his sole authority. In addition, communication, in this pre-radio age, was rather problematic, and so it was not always easy to keep in touch with key parts of the battlefield, vitally important though that was. So instead of an enveloping action to the west of Paris, Kluck now took a direct line to the south-east. He did this in order to deal with the threat he deemed coming from the French army. And soon Kluck's determination to finish the war as soon as possible resulted in his army, the First, being even further away from where the original plan had intended.

Joffre was now able to show what true flexibility was able to achieve. He had already given an army to Gallieni in order to defend Paris, thereby jettisoning his original plans to fight the Germans elsewhere. Then he was helped by the intervention of Field Marshal Lord Kitchener, now Secretary of State for War in London. Sir John French, the

BEF commander, had doubts on the capacity of France to continue resistance. This Kitchener deemed to be defeatist: French had his orders to stay with the French!

By September 4th, with one German army miles from where it was intended to be and the British now firmly ready to defend France to the utmost, Joffre launched his own plan of counter-attack. He ordered his armies north and east, to take on the German invaders. The Battle of the Ourcq on September 5th showed that the French could take on the enemy without losing. Gallieni also moved the army now under his command against Kluck's forces. Once more the taxi drivers of Paris rallied to the city's defence by taking as many troops to the front as possible.

The Battle of the Marne was now fully under way. General Ferdinand Foch, the intrepid commander of the French Ninth Army, uttered what were to become famous words: 'My centre is giving way, my right is falling back, situation excellent, I attack.'

All along this front the French and British were fighting back. Soon Bülow and his army were in retreat. This was not according to the German plan, and Moltke, unable to find out himself what was going on, now controversially dispatched a staff officer, Lieutenant Colonel Richard Hentsch, to find out on his behalf. In normal circumstances this would have been a wholly rational thing to do. Hentsch's mission has only become disputed because of what followed as the result of his report – a general German withdrawal. Since Hentsch was to die during the war, he was unable to be interviewed after it.

Consequently the Hentsch investigation became a scapegoat for those Germans looking for reasons why the long-expected defeat of France never happened. Moltke, edging ever nearer to a serious nervous breakdown, also gave Hentsch complete powers to issue orders in Moltke's name should the circumstances so demand. Bülow was finished anyway, but Kluck had wanted to press on, regardless of how exposed he would thereby have rendered German troops under his command. However, Hentsch, exercising his authority from Moltke, now ordered Kluck to retreat as well.

The offensive that had begun with the Schlieffen Plan and the invasion of Belgium was now all but over. German forces retreated to the River Aisne, where they began to dig the trenches that would soon become notorious for the next four years. Attack had led to stalemate, a situation that despite the loss of millions of lives would not be resolved until the Hundred Days' Offensive of 1918 and the arrival of the army from the USA.

Moltke's personal resolve now disintegrated into what we would today recognise as a serious psychological breakdown. He resigned his command over all the German armies informally on September 14th and was formally dismissed as Chief of Staff on November 3rd. He died in much sorrow of a heart attack in 1916, having never really recovered from the debacle of what was supposed to have been a great German triumph, of the kind his uncle had achieved against the French in 1870.

Debate on the Schlieffen Plan has raged ever since the Germans failed to capture Paris. After 1918, many blamed Germany's defeat on the adjustments made to the Plan by Moltke. But could the Schlieffen Plan possibly have succeeded?

Some academics argue that the Plan was played around with so much that what finally happened when it was launched for real in August 1914 made its name meaningless. Huge rows have erupted among scholars on whether or not the Germans put too much emphasis, for example, on the left side of the attack, rather than on the right, as Schlieffen himself is said to have requested on his deathbed.

But others, not necessarily academics, have asked what is surely a legitimate question: regardless of any tweaks made by subsequent German commanders, could even the original plan have succeeded?

Here one could argue that the answer must be 'no'. Allan Mallinson, the writer and a former army staff officer himself, notes, as do other writers, the fact that even the slightest delay on what was a very rigid timetable could throw the whole plan awry. The delays that happened in real life once war began show this. Historian David Stevenson, meanwhile, has pointed out what are certainly the deeply grave 'logistical shortcomings inherent in the Schlieffen-Moltke Plan'. Communications, for example, were terrible, and by September the Germans were getting so frantic that they were sending radio messages *en clair*. This meant that the British and French could intercept and read them with ease.

It is above all in the logistics of the Plan that it all comes unstuck. We forget logistics at our peril, especially if our concentration is on individual battles and the grand strategy of leaders. Stevenson, for example, writes:

> Beyond the frontier railheads the troops had to march with heavy packs and chafing boots in sweltering heat, Kluck's men covering 500 kilometres in a month. Men or horses had to carry the supplies, as the entire German army was disposed of only 4,000 lorries and before it reached the Marne 60 per cent of them broke down.

The Germans needed horses, but, if anything, a horse needs more forage than a human being needs food. By the time of Kluck's adventures near Paris, what matters more than whether or not he went to the west or to the south-east of the capital is this set of facts:

Kluck's 84,000 horses needed 2 million pounds of fodder a day, the roads being strewn with dying animals and the heavy guns left behind. Nor could the Germans make good their losses in men, as soldiers dropped from exhaustion as well as wounds. By September many units were down to half their initial strength.

Not only that, but by the time Moltke realised that retreat was the only possible option, Kluck's army was eighty miles distant from its nearest supply railhead and Bülow's unfortunate soldiers some one hundred miles away.

So could the Germans have won if they had stayed loyal to the Schlieffen Plan and followed it down to the very last letter? Perhaps not. Plans are one thing but reality is another. With the delays from Liège onwards, with the arrival of the British BEF, and with the hideous logistical problems inevitable for an army that uses horses and demands that soldiers walk vast distances on foot, the Schlieffen Plan simply seems to lack all credibility.

The cost to all the soldiers involved in this particular battle was massive. There were, it has been estimated, around 220,000 German casualties, a slightly higher 250,000 French casualties (of whom 80,000 were deaths) and around 13,000 for the BEF (including 1,700 who died). In later battles far more soldiers were to die than in what has been called the 'First Battle of the Marne'. But the rate of injuries and deaths *per day* as an average were to remain some of the highest of the war.

Four years of hideous attrition in the trenches now lay ahead. But the key thing was that none of those 250,000 French soldiers killed or injured had suffered in vain. 1914 was no 1870 and France had *not* been defeated. The Germans had failed.

And that failure changed the entire outcome of the war. For as other conflicts were to show, Germany could not in effect fight a war on two fronts. It would be simply too much even for a nation as militarily or economically powerful. So one could, albeit controversially, say that with the failure of the Schlieffen Plan eventual German defeat was certain, sooner or later. And in 1918, such was indeed to be the case.

THE SIEGE OF KUT

December 7th 1914–April 29th 1915

If asked to name the worst defeat of the Allies in World
War I most people would probably answer 'Gallipoli'. But
they would be wrong – the British defeat at the siege of Kut
from December 1914 to April 1915 was far worse, not just
in terms of the immediate death toll. There is also the fact
that the Turks treated their prisoners of war so badly that
over 4,000 British and Indian prisoners died in captivity,
many of them in the walk through the desert, after capture,
to Aleppo in Syria.

Jan Morris in *Farewell the Trumpets* has called Kut the
'most abject capitulation in Britain's military history'.
While the surrender of Singapore in 1942 could match
it for ignominy, there is a point to be made. Racism

towards the Turkish troops was both completely unacceptable and a military mistake. Regrettably the British commander in Mesopotamia in 1914, General Charles Townshend, felt his imperial forces to be invincible against the Turks.

So when he launched his invasion of what we would now call Iraq, from the recently captured port of Basra, he thought that he could get all the way to the key Ottoman city of Baghdad without difficulty. His army consisted of both British and Indian Empire forces, and within a few weeks he was within sight of that legendary city itself.

But Townshend had, in his arrogance, massively overextended his troops, and he was now a dangerously long distance from his supply base in Basra. Not only that, but at Ctesiphon, the former capital of the ancient Sassanid civilisation just outside Baghdad, he was forced by Ottoman forces to make a tactical retreat. Instead of going all the way back to a place not too far away from Basra, which is on the coast, he stopped at the town of Kut, an easily defended semi-island on a U-bend on the left bank of the Tigris. Here he thought he could stay with his army until he was rescued.

However, he was to be proved disastrously wrong. He was too far from Basra to be reached easily, and between December 1914 and April 1915 no fewer than three relief expeditions all failed to lift the siege – the final attempt under General George Gorringe in early April, involving over 30,000 soldiers, proving as much a disaster as the others.

In the end, British and Indian casualties came to over 23,000 killed or wounded. So desperate did the situation become that the imperial authorities even attempted to bribe the Turks to release the garrison. Both T. E. Lawrence ('Lawrence of Arabia') and the adventurer Aubrey Herbert (the inspiration for the character in John Buchan's novel *Greenmantle*) were employed as intermediaries. All failed.

As a result the garrison was forced to surrender. Townshend was taken to luxurious captivity in Constantinople and survived the war. But thousands of ordinary soldiers died of thirst or starvation in the desert. The contrast in the way privileged and regular prisoners were treated appalled everyone.

The outcome of the campaign was changed when the British government took direct control of Mesopotamia from that of the Raj in India. As we shall see, in March 1917, under the more experienced command of General Sir Frederick Maude, Baghdad was captured.

Today we remember Maude but forget Townshend and the 4,000 who died shamefully ill-treated in captivity. Perhaps the reason can be found in the reaction of the political boss of Kut, Austen Chamberlain (Secretary of State for India responsible for the Indian Raj) – he took his responsibility on the chin, resigned, never made a fuss and regained office not long later without a loss of face. Today Austen Chamberlain, who narrowly failed to become prime minister in 1922, is forgotten. So too is Kut, which, if not the worst disaster in British military history, was most certainly an ignominious and unnecessary defeat.

A WORLD AT WAR

East Africa and East Asia, 1914 Onwards

The original name for World War I was the 'Great War', since the very notion of so terrible a conflict ever happening again was unthinkable until it actually happened in 1939. Even then for a while people would refer to the Great War and to the World War. It was only later, and in retrospect, that these events became what we call them today: the First World War and the Second World War.

Much of the first conflict took place in the Middle East. Therefore it was certainly not just a European war. But, unlike its successor, most of the first war, and the worst bloodshed, occurred on the Western and Eastern Fronts within Europe. However, some of the fighting also took place in the areas surrounding German colonies. These were German East Africa (what became Tanganyika under British rule along with Rwanda and Burundi), German South-West Africa (now Namibia), German Papua New Guinea (now part of the country of the same name, united with the Australian-ruled portion) and the German-ruled ports surrounded by Chinese territory in East Asia. Many other small German territories existed around the globe, including some small island groups in the Pacific and in West Africa (now Cameroon and Togo).

In the Pacific, ANZAC (Australian New Zealand Army Corps) forces took the various islands swiftly, without much resistance, and Papua surrendered without a fight to the Australians on September 17th 1914.

Tsingtao, the German treaty port (with a similar status to the British-ruled Hong Kong) was seized by both Japanese and British troops. Japan declared war on Germany on August 21st 1914, and a small number of Japanese troops were to fight in the Middle East alongside the Australian and New Zealand forces under British command. In Tsingtao there was considerable resistance, with 200 German defenders killed and 1,455 Japanese deaths.

Togo surrendered swiftly, whereas Cameroon proved much harder, with some 25,000 Allied troops needed to subdue the Germans. Not until 1916 was the latter colony finally conquered and unusually the region was shared between Britain and France after 1918. Consequently

Cameroon is a French-speaking British Commonwealth country today.

The most exciting and well-known conflict was in German East Africa, at this point split into three areas – the mainland (Tanganyika) portion of today's Tanzania, and the two small states of what were then called Ruanda and Urundi, the latter also well known for its large numbers of British Church of England missionaries.

In that conflict in East Africa the Germans were lucky in their local commander, Paul von Lettow-Vorbeck (usually just called von Lettow). He was an excellent guerrilla fighter, so much so that he was still fighting the British even for a short while after Armistice Day on November 11th 1918. Historian John Keegan has rightly described von Lettow as someone who 'with Lawrence of Arabia [was] one of the few truly individualist leaders of the First World War'.

What made von Lettow special is that although he was a white Western colonialist he persuaded many Africans to stay loyal to Germany and to fight under his command. These troops were named 'askaris' and they proved some of the best guerrillas of the war. At one stage von Lettow was so successful that even an Allied force as large as 350,000 troops plus local African porters was unable to capture him and his askaris. In 1916 the British appointed their former Boer war enemy, General Jan Smuts, as their own commander in the area for some of the war, but although he had personal experience of fighting the British as a guerrilla himself, not even he could crush von Lettow. Not until November 25th 1918 did von Lettow finally surrender.

In South-West Africa the situation was somewhat different, as prior to 1914 the Germans had committed probably the worst atrocities against the local population of any of the European colonial powers in Africa. Despite the vast size of the country – roughly six times bigger than England – only about 80,000 local peoples lived there. These were the survivors. Between 1904 and 1907 the Germans are estimated to have slaughtered up to half the original inhabitants in what is rightly called a campaign of genocide. There would be no askaris in South-West Africa.

The British were determined to conquer the region as fast as possible. This was politically delicate as the country bordered not just on the British colonies in southern Africa (such as today's Botswana) but also on the Union of South Africa. This federation was the outcome of the Boer War in which the Dutch colonists of Transvaal and the Orange Free State had fought the British of Cape Colony, and in which the British had often treated the Dutch 'Boers' very badly. No one was quite sure how the Boer/Dutch survivors in 1914 would feel about a British campaign against the Boers' erstwhile encourager, Germany.

Some Boers did indeed rebel, only swiftly to be crushed by Boers loyal to the United Kingdom and to actual British troops. By July 9th 1915 all German and Boer resistance had crumbled. Unfortunately for the inhabitants of South-West

Africa, this region was to be given to the Union of South Africa after 1918, so that the subsequent apartheid regime did not grant independence to Namibia until years after other former colonies such as Zambia and Botswana had gained their freedom.

Hundreds of thousands of Western or Western-led African soldiers fought in this conflict. This inevitably meant that in Europe, British or French officers whose presence in Flanders or France would have been invaluable were fighting a colonial war thousands of miles away. For Africans or for those inhabiting other German colonies, thousands of them were fighting a war for colonial masters whom none of them had chosen. Not only that, but the diseases endemic in Africa also took a dreadful toll, with over 600,000 Allied soldiers and their civilian porters dying from illness during the conflict. It was a terrible price.

PART TWO

WAR IN THE TRENCHES

THE BATTLE OF NEUVE-CHAPELLE

March 10th–13th 1915

From the start of 1915 right through until the Hundred Days of 1918, when the Americans and the tank came to the rescue, countless futile attempts were made by both British and French commanders to achieve a strategic breakthrough on the Western Front. All of them failed, and some were to become infamous, battles in which hundreds of thousands of soldiers died in vain just to capture a few yards of enemy land.

But the 'lions led by donkeys' description of all these scenes of carnage is perhaps unfair. No British or French general wanted simply to sacrifice needlessly the lives of millions of their own side. Apart from anything else, such gargantuan losses could result in defeat. As the Allies were painfully aware, their replacement levels compared to Germany's were not great, so that lives lost in assaults on the trenches could not be made up even when compulsory conscription came into effect, which it did in 1916.

Generals such as Haig on the British side and, later on, Nivelle and Foch on the French were always trying to think of new ways to beat the enemy, shorten the war and create victory for the Allies with no further loss of life. It is just that they really had no idea what best to do – and nor did anyone else. Even a general with a deep sense of compassion for his troops could have done no better than the harder-hearted commanders like Haig under whom so many had to suffer. Direct assault on the enemy trenches was the only way that *anyone* knew, Allied or German alike.

In 1915 the British army still consisted of professionals who had joined up voluntarily, and so economy with lives, even disregarding the emotional impact of casualties, was important. In March there existed a possibility that 40,000 British troops could attack a small German salient at a place called Neuve-Chapelle. Aerial reconnaissance, then in its infancy, was even used to ensure success. When the British bombardment began on the morning of March 10th, it looked briefly as if the plan might possibly work. The Germans were caught entirely by surprise and the British, temporarily, were able to make substantial gains.

But then the assault stopped. Communications proved distinctly shaky and by the time that the British had regrouped, German troops from the rear had been able to come forward, counter-attack and propel them all the way back. And worse still, the BEF troops had run out of ammunition.

What happened to ordinary soldiers at this battle was to be similar to countless equally tragic tales as the trench warfare of the Western Front became the norm. The following quotation, from a sixtieth anniversary of victory compilation in 1978, epitomises what it was like for the ordinary soldier.

'[A] bullet pierced the exact centre of the helmet of the man on my right,' one veteran recalled, 'as he walked forward with his head down. He spun round as he fell with a stream of blood spurting out of a circular hole in the top of his head, and he scrambled back for about ten yards then rolled over. A short, white-haired lad rushed screaming, right along our line with an eye shot away. Another neighbour was hit in the groin and lay in the ditch at the foot of the slope screaming.'

Remember that far worse was to come than this. During the whole of the conflict there was none of the psychological support mechanism for soldiers then that exists now. In addition, these soldiers were for the most part volunteers who had joined after the war began, not professionals who had seen death before. Most people signing up in 1914 had expected the war to end by that Christmas, but now here they were, in 1915, and with not the remotest possibility of an end in sight. By 1917 French losses were to cause mutinies. But what is extraordinary is that the British – along with Canadian, Australian, New Zealand, South African and Indian troops – all persevered right down until victory, without any mutiny or collective breakdown. In view of the traumas that even the survivors faced upon a daily basis, this is really astonishing and a tribute to the sheer courage of hundreds of thousands of soldiers who were in effect civilians in uniform.

Haig was puzzled at the failure of the assault. One analysis argues that the real problem – one that was to last most of the rest of the war – was that British commanders felt that there had been inadequate bombardment of the German positions. The answer in future would be much bigger artillery bombardments, which would ideally flatten enemy positions and thus allow Allied forces more easily to capture German lines.

However, such an earth-shattering preliminary always removed the element of surprise. Since it was the shock of seeing British troops unexpectedly that had caused the initial German confusion at Neuve-Chapelle, then perhaps the British commanders were learning the wrong lesson from what had gone awry.

John Keegan, though, the doyen of military studies for

many years at the Royal Military Academy at Sandhurst, has what is arguably a much more substantial and nuanced view. This is worth quoting in full because it explains *all* the failures of 1915–1918, including, above all, that of the Somme in 1916, the worst debacle in the history of the British army.

When it comes to Neuve Chapelle, he writes, all 'the contributing factors that were to bedevil success in trench offensives for much of the war were present, both the functional and structural'. Taking a more pessimistic view of the impact of the tank than many would, he goes on to say that the 'functional were to be cured, in time, the structural persisted, even after the development and large-scale deployment of the tank in 1917'.

What he calls the 'functional' failures were the 'inadequacy of artillery support, rigidity of planning, mispositioning of the reserves and lack of delegation in command'.

On the 'structural' side the mistakes were 'the relative immobility and total vulnerability to fire of the advancing infantry and absence of means of speedy communication between front and rear, between infantry and artillery and between neighbouring units'.

One of the worst of these failures was the utter lack of telephone/radio technology between the attacking soldiers and the commanders in the rear. The successful British at Neuve-Chapelle, for instance, had no safe way of telling their senior officers that they had achieved the first objective and could thus press on to the next goal. All too often in the war, soldiers were to achieve an objective and then be forced to wait for further instructions, during which time, as at Neuve-Chapelle, the enemy could regroup and counter-attack. Runners were often the only way of getting information back to headquarters, a method no different from those used in ancient Roman times!

Keegan thus concludes that 'the unfolding of action at Neuve-Chapelle demonstrates the operation of all these factors as if in a military laboratory'. The tragedy of the next three years was that these lessons were to be learnt at hideous expense, at the cost of millions of lives.

Neuve-Chapelle has one sad claim to fame. The Germans used fragmentation gas shells in the battle. While far worse poisons were to emerge during the war, notably the employment of chlorine gas, Neuve-Chapelle was one of the first instances in the conflict in which this kind of weapon was used.

THE BATTLE OF GALLIPOLI

March 18th 1915–January 9th 1916

The attempt to end World War I prematurely by launching a daring invasion of Constantinople, the Ottoman capital, is one of the most written about episodes of World War I. The idea was to send a naval and military force through the Dardanelles, then through the Bosphorus, and then to capture Constantinople. The Dardanelles is the narrow strait through which one has to pass to enter the Bosphorus Sea and thence Constantinople and the Black Sea. These two straits separate mainland Europe and Asia and are the key to control of the Black Sea. March 18th is a compromise date for the start of operations as some begin them in April 1915 or even as early as February that year.

This invasion, known as the Dardanelles or Gallipoli Campaign, is also famous for two other reasons. First, it was in essence the brainchild of Winston Churchill, at the outset First Lord of the Admiralty and the politician in charge of the Royal Navy. Churchill has often been applauded for his maverick genius; in the Second World War this became one of his most loveable attributes. His support for wayward and profoundly oddball scientists who came up with weird but ultimately brilliant ideas became legendary. The First World War was no exception. Although not directly responsible for the invention of the tank, the weapon that above all helped gain victory against Germany in 1918, he was closely instrumental in encouraging its development, both as First Lord of the Admiralty, and, later in the war, as Minister of Munitions.

But for every stroke of genius like the tank would be an equivalent hare-brained idea that would either be overruled or, in the case of Gallipoli, lead to utter disaster. One such scheme was to seize the Frisian island of Borkum, attack Germany from the north, and force the Netherlands into the war. Thankfully this scheme was squashed by all his advisers and never happened. Nevertheless, for years the debacle and sense of shame at so massive a defeat at Gallipoli haunted him and thus his entire reputation. He would write works of self-vindication obsessively and so it became one of the best known parts of the war, not just for what happened but also for his vigorous defence of it.

The events also coincided with Australia becoming legally a fully united country, so that people who left, say as Tasmanians or Queenslanders, returned as Australians. The death of so many Australians and New Zealanders in the ANZAC division also became a focus of unity in both countries, each only recently independent – more so in the former than in the latter nation. The deaths of so many fine young men, thousands of miles from home, in a military disaster, has been singed into the Australian national consciousness in a way similar to the Battle of the Somme in Britain.

Since Australians fought with considerable distinction in some of the finest victories of the war, and did so under excellent commanders, this concentration on defeat and sorrow might seem strange to outsiders. But the idea of 'mateship' (mateyness) that runs strongly in the Australian national psyche was powerfully expressed through the common suffering in the trenches at Gallipoli. So perhaps, from that perspective, it is not so odd after all.

Gallipoli was part of a much wider debate that raged in Allied councils throughout the war. How could Germany be defeated? One massive assault after another against enemy positions in Flanders seemed only to pile up bodies, and lead to one scene of carnage and frustration after another. So a school of thought emerged that saw attacking Germany's less able allies in the rear as a way forward, of getting around the impassable trenches in Flanders and at the enemy from another direction. Those who advocated this approach were nicknamed 'Easterners', as they favoured using the countries to the east of Germany (Turkey, Bulgaria, Austria-Hungary) as a way through to victory.

The Battle of Gallipoli thus came to be placed within the context of a much larger debate. To the military, troops taken away from Flanders meant fewer soldiers with which to fight the Germans on the Western Front. To the Easterners, schemes such as Churchill's were the only possibility of victory that avoided the carnage of Flanders and the trenches.

In 1915 the Russians were in serious need of an alternative supply route. The best way would be through the Dardanelles, but with Turkey's entry into the war on Germany's side this became impossible. Serbia was also in grave danger from Austria, and now Bulgaria was thinking of joining the Central Powers to make up for its losses in the Second Balkan War. The case for the Easterners thus began to grow by the day, especially as the Allied forces now had soldiers based nearby. France was keen for Greece to enter the war, and to this end had deposited an army (which included some British troops) in the Greek town of Salonika, today's Thessaloniki. In addition, Britain had a large army in Egypt to guard the Suez Canal – then the vital sea route to India.

The carnage in Flanders had come as a huge shock to many of the politicians, who had clearly never learnt the lessons of the American Civil War: that with modern technology large-scale death becomes increasingly inevitable. So when in early 1915 Churchill's eager eyes fell upon the Dardanelles as a way of knocking the Ottoman Empire out of the war, he was now playing to a receptive audience.

It should never be forgotten that Kitchener too, the iconic Secretary of State for War, was also very open to the idea. Without his agreement it would never have got off the ground, and in many ways he was as much to blame for the subsequent debacle as Churchill himself. But Kitchener was a national hero ten feet above contradiction. Then in 1916 he was to die in a torpedoed ship at sea, out of the picture and remembered only for his victories.

To begin with, Churchill thought that a naval bombardment could do the trick on its own. On March 18th 1915, mainly with old ships but with one significant modern dreadnought, *Queen Elizabeth*, the serious naval bombardment began, along with an attempt to 'force the narrows' (that is, to shoot their way through the Dardanelles) and blast through to Constantinople itself. However, the minesweepers that the British possessed were utterly useless, and soon the British had lost three major ships in the attempt to bombard the fortifications and ram their way through the Straits.

As historian David Stevenson is surely right to add: what if the ships had actually made it all the way through to Constantinople? It would hardly have induced the Turks to surrender. A naval bombardment on its own could never have been enough.

The naval attack also warned the Turks that the British (and French) were thinking of extending military operations to the Dardanelles. The fortifications were therefore strengthened under the able German commander General Otto Liman von Sanders. The Ottoman forces now had among them Mustafa Kemal, one of the ablest of their officers, and who later on, as Kemal Atatürk, was to become one of the most successful Turkish leaders of recent centuries.

The British commander, by contrast, was General Sir Ian Hamilton, whom posterity remembers as one of Britain's most incompetent wartime leaders. It took a whole month for the British, French and ANZAC forces to arrive, so that any remote element of surprise that might have existed had long since vanished. Correlli Barnett is right to argue that the only faint chance of success would have been what we now call a 'combined operation' of the kind that did so well on D-Day in 1944, with the naval bombardment and military landings taking place simultaneously. But with these two events being a month apart, the operation was in essence doomed from the start. Not until April 1915 did the land invasion begin.

Only one part of the landing force consisted of experienced professional soldiers, and the rest, British and ANZAC alike, were raw recruits hurled mercilessly onto a hostile shore. Indeed, one of the bays upon which Allied troops landed was so hostile that it had not been guarded by the Turks, since the defenders presumed that so impossible a landing beach would never be used by the invaders.

Thousands of Allied soldiers died within minutes of landing, and the only troops to advance any distance were soon turned back. It is important to remember that among the many dead were not just Australian and New Zealander but also English, many Irish and not a few French as well.

Within days of attempting to land, the Allied forces were obliged to dig trenches, so that one set of murderous trenches in Flanders was substituted for equally dangerous equivalents on the Gallipoli side of the Dardanelles. Further, while Allied troops in Western Europe had a hinterland to which to get back for comfort and rest, that option was not open to those in Gallipoli. The two areas they occupied, Cape Helles and Suvla Bay, were right on the sea. There was no escape from their suffering. The weather was terrible, especially as the heat of summer made life intolerable for those unused to such humidity. Even worse, many recalled, were the flies. This last torment became a famous poem by the writer A. P. Herbert:

> The flies! Oh God, the flies
> That soiled the sacred dead,
> To see them swarm from dead men's eyes,
> And share the soldiers' bread!
> Nor think I now forget
> The filth and stench of war,
> The corpses on the parapet,
> The maggots in the floor.

By late summer, seventy-eight per cent of ANZACS suffered from dysentery and over sixty per cent from heat sores. An attempt in August to break out failed, and by October the incompetent Sir Ian, who stayed mainly on the ship *Queen Elizabeth*, away from all the unpleasantness, was replaced with General Sir Charles Monro.

The latter realised that the situation had now become totally hopeless, which common sense would have indicated had been true from the beginning. He recommended the only realistic course available, which was to evacuate.

On November 12th–15th Kitchener himself visited, and discovered that in the new cold winter conditions over 15,000 men were now suffering from frostbite. He too agreed that evacuation was the only solution to a failed mission. Winston Churchill, who had been ousted from the Admiralty back in May, now resigned from the government altogether, his political career, he feared, now finished, aged only forty-one.

Thankfully the evacuation, which took place between December 1915 and January 1916, was the one success of the whole operation, astonishingly with no losses at all. The campaign was now over.

Many of the British Empire casualties died from illness rather than from battle combat. These losses include, for example, the poet Rupert Brooke. Including deaths from disease as well as battle, the injured and the evacuated sick, British Empire casualties came to some 205,000 people – plus a further and often forgotten 47,000 French. In theory the Turks had lost a quarter of a million soldiers, but many suspect that the actual figures were far higher. Of the thousands who died, over 34,000 were British, nearly 10,000 French and just under 9,000 Australian. But while over three times as many Britons died as Australians, it is Australia that most remembers Gallipoli. ANZAC Day remains a sacred and shared national memory there today.

Churchill's political career eventually recovered, after a period of direct military service on the Western Front near a town called Ploegsteert (or 'Plugstreet' to give its British nickname). But he never forgot the lessons of Gallipoli. One of the most important innovations of his time as prime minister in the Second World War was something that we take for granted today but which was then wholly new: *Combined Operations*. This involved the three services combining together for joint plans on how to fight the war as a unified whole. As mentioned earlier, D-Day was the ultimate achievement of such an approach.

So the soldiers who died in their thousands on the fly-ridden beaches of Gallipoli may never have taken Constantinople. But in terms of lessons learnt, they had most certainly not died in vain.

THE SECOND BATTLE OF YPRES

April 22nd–May 25th 1915

Four battles were fought near the historic Belgian town of Ypres, the third of which in 1917 is usually referred to as Passchendaele. Ypres would soon find its way into British folklore as 'Wipers', the average soldier being unable to pronounce unfamiliar Belgian names. From 1916 to 1918 there was to be a satirical newspaper produced by one of the regiments, the Sherwood Foresters, called the *Wipers Times*.

The first battle, however, took place in October–November 1914, when hope was still alive in the Allied armies that the Germans could be driven back out of Belgian territory. Most of the troops, on both sides, still held out hope for a speedy victory.

This was to prove sadly optimistic. The stalemate that

was to characterise the Allies on one side and Germany on the other was not to change until 1918. At the First Battle of Ypres Britain, France and Belgium sustained well over 130,000 casualties (killed, wounded or 'missing') and Germany approximately the same. For the Germans it was especially traumatic, since some 25,000 volunteers of student age were among the dead. Tragically, as the campaigns of attrition in the trenches had begun, so they would continue.

In April 1915 the Germans had discovered that their Austro-Hungarian ally on the Eastern Front was an increasingly broken reed. It was thus necessary to transfer some eleven divisions to that front from Flanders. This had to be achieved in a way that disguised the move. (Those who transferred were to be victorious, at the Battle of Gorlice-Tarnów.) In order to accomplish this, the High Command ordered an attack on the Ypres salient, scene of the earlier battle.

In the battle for Warsaw in January 1915 the Germans had begun to experiment with poison gas. In that first instance the tear gas had proven doubly ineffective, as it had not worried the Russian victims and because the strong winter temperatures had frozen the gas. Now in April they had a far more powerful poison, one based upon chlorine, and Ypres would be the testing ground. Soon the hideous effects would become apparent, with the lungs of the victims so filled with the fluid produced that they drowned. The Germans had 6,000 cylinders of gas, weighing over 160 tons, ready to unleash.

Strictly speaking, what we call Second Ypres was around six battles fought over a period of as many weeks. The initial battle began on April 22nd as the grey-green gas cloud floated towards the French trenches. All the Allied forces, including for the first time a division of Canadian troops, were subject as well to the usual ear-shattering artillery bombardment with which each new offensive now began. The Germans also tried to use gas again in further attacks. However, the Allies swiftly found, in the days before proper gas masks, that to soak cloth in cold water and put the wet rag around the mouth could often be an effective form of defence.

In May, the British and French did their best to counter-attack. The French briefly seized Vimy Ridge, which would later become famous as the site of a Canadian victory. But overall this failed to penetrate the German lines sufficiently to dislodge them permanently. The one good result was that the town of Ypres remained in Allied hands, as would continue to be the case throughout the war. The famous medieval Cloth Hall Tower of Ypres was shattered. But the fact that anything was left of the original at all was a symbolic reminder of Allied defiance against the German invaders.

THE BATTLE AND CAMPAIGN OF GORLICE-TARNÓW

May 1st–September 19th 1915

The Battles of Tannenberg and of the Masurian Lakes in 1914 had given Germany a massive superiority over the Russians. By contrast, the Austro-Hungarian forces in the Carpathians had been routed and routed again by the Russians. In addition, the very security of the Habsburg realms was itself threatened by the Russian successes. It became obvious that the Austro-Hungarian forces could not beat Russia on their own, especially since they were now in effect fighting a three-front war, against not just Russia but also Italy and Serbia. In 1914 the Kingdom of Italy had been theoretically linked to the Austro-Hungarian Empire. But many in the Empire were of Italian origin and had no wish to continue as Austrian subjects. It was not surprising that in 1915 Britain and France were able to bribe Italy to change sides.

German aid became necessary, and in May 1915, when battle recommenced, it included a German-Austrian army under one of the German victors in East Prussia, General August von Mackensen.

The Gorlice-Tarnów area was to the south-east of Cracow, a city now famous for being the town of *Schindler's List* in Poland, but in 1915 part of the Austro-Hungarian Empire. The plan itself was Austrian, the firepower, in the form of over a million shells to be unleashed over a thirty-mile front, was German.

As historians have noted ruefully, Mackensen's tactics against the Russians were to be exactly those of the victorious Allies in 1918: 'deep penetration by the infantry and a rapid follow-up by the artillery'. The initial bombardment on May 1st wiped out the Russian positions. By May 13th the Central Powers had reached Przemyśl, whose castle became an Austrian fortress after being in Russian hands.

Due to the way in which the former Poland was carved up in 1815, Warsaw was a Russian city. But now, by August 4th, it was captured by the German and Austro-Hungarian forces. By September 4th they were in historic Russia itself, with four of the most important frontier fortresses – Kovno (in modern Lithuania) and Brest-Litovsk (now in Belarus) among them – in their hands.

The German/Austrian troops had been successful beyond their wildest dreams. But they now disagreed on what to do next. Some Germans wanted their victorious forces transferred to the Western Front. The Austrians, deeply concerned about their new front against Italy, wished for troops to be transferred to that area. And Mackensen simply wanted to continue his victory roll. His view prevailed.

However, sharp minds remembered an event of 1812 – a victorious invading commander massively overextending his lines of communication and entering into deep Russian territory, only to lose to the sheer overwhelming size of Russia's landmass. Napoleon might have captured Moscow but he was to lose the war. By September the very forces of nature that defeated Napoleon, and were to go on to destroy Hitler in 1941–1945, were already at work. The uniquely Russian *rasputitsa,* or the semi-annual mud season, had now begun, making transportation logistics for invading armies a nightmare.

And then there was the other factor that defeated both Napoleon and Hitler – the unending ability of the Russian army to replace itself because of the colossal size of the Russian population (then including what is now the Ukraine and Belarus, the Baltic states and the new nations in Central Asia). Losses that would have crippled or destroyed other countries could be borne by

Russia in a way that was impossible for anyone else.

By the beginning of September, taking all its fronts into account – Russian forces were fighting Turkey in the Caucasus as well as Germany and the Austro-Hungarian Empire – the Russian Empire had lost *a million* soldiers killed or injured and 750,000 had been captured by their enemies. Yet despite all this they still had reserves of somewhere over eighteen million, of whom no less than four million were ready for call-up in 1916–1917. However many Russians the Germans and their allies were able to kill, there were always far more to replace them than those who had died.

Russia might therefore have lost its Polish territory, and was later to go on to lose the Baltic region that Tsar Peter the Great had captured from Sweden back in the seventeenth century. But however grievous its losses, and whatever the magnitude of victory for Germany/Austria-Hungary in the Gorlice-Tarnów campaign, the war continued.

So who won this battle? The Germans had been able to prevent their Austro-Hungarian ally from going down to defeat. Vast territories and fortresses had been taken. But Russia remained undefeated, ready to fight another day, as Napoleon had discovered in 1812.

THE BATTLE OF LOOS

September 25th–October 14th 1915

1915 should have been a good year for the Allies, with the accession of Italy to their ranks. But in fact, despite some successes on the Russian Front, it was in reality more of the same – a war of attrition.

This is not what it should have been all about. The British commanders were, as historian John Keegan has so accurately observed, still essentially 'colonial' in outlook, fighting natives in distant parts, with rapid movement over wide spaces. Trench warfare, into which the Allies had become stuck, was by its very nature entirely different, with the defenders normally having the advantage over the attackers. This was not how the British were used to fighting, and until the technical breakthroughs of 1918 – and the arrival of hundreds of thousands of fresh American soldiers from the USA the same year – nothing really changed to alter that basic fact of modern war.

The Battle of Loos, on the French side of the border with Belgium, began for the British on September 25th 1915. The troops went forward almost as if on parade ground, straight into accurate German machine-gun fire, in an area the defenders swiftly nicknamed 'the corpse field of Loos'. One German machine gun fired 12,500 rounds in a 'single afternoon' and the defenders were able to counter oncoming British attackers at between 200 and 1500 yards, all with ease. On the first day alone, 8,000 British soldiers were killed or injured, and so horrified were the Germans at the death toll by the next day that the machine gunners decided not to fire as the survivors straggled back to their trenches.

Interestingly, the British meanwhile were using poison gas against the enemy. It was mainly the German forces that used gas during the war, but at Loos it was employed by Britain, and with terrible side effects, as the wind blew much of the gas back onto the British trenches. While only three per cent of the overall death toll in World War I was gas-related, it was a dreadful and inhumane weapon to use and it was outlawed in the 1920s, one of the very few restrictions in battle to which Hitler kept in the Second World War.

By the time that the fighting ceased around October 13th, some 16,000 British soldiers had lost their lives. The French soldiers had a far worse time. For an equal lack of permanent success they suffered over 143,000 casualties killed or injured by October 31st. And as one historian sadly notes, the 'German line was scarcely penetrated'. As usual, German casualties are hard to gauge but they were nowhere near as bad as those of the British or French. Many lives had been lost ostensibly for nothing.

Due to these disasters, Sir John French was dismissed as commander of the BEF, to be replaced by General Sir Douglas Haig.

A winner in terms of British command, Sir Douglas Haig was, as we shall discover, a deeply controversial choice, praised to the skies in more recent times but loathed by many, both during the war itself and in the years following, when he became the convenient scapegoat for the slaughter in the trenches.

But in fairness to Haig, and perhaps even to French, it was Lord Kitchener who informed his reluctant commanders that they should be prepared for heavy casualties in pursuit of Allied aims. And it was France's senior general, Joffre, who really thought that the Germans could actually be pushed back by Allied offensive action, certainly in terms of removing the enemy salient (the 'Noyon Bulge') that seemed to stretch too near to Paris for comfort.

Still, Haig's successful intrigue to replace Sir John French as BEF commander would ultimately make no difference, since the battles which erupted in the following year were to make 1915's casualties look low in comparison. The war on the Western Front was to get far worse, under the 'shadow of the Somme'.

The Battle of the Somme in 1916 was to cause much soul-searching both then and since. But in terms of basic tactics of attack and attrition, there was in reality not much difference between the two battles, except that in the Somme the casualties and death toll were to be horrifically and exponentially higher.

Loos was a battle of attrition that should, in normal circumstances, have stopped after the carnage of the first two days, when it became clear that the British were not going to make a serious impact on the German lines. Firing Sir John French was not the answer. But, tragically for the old Tommies who had survived 1914, and the first wave of the new Kitchener recruits of 1915, there was no other realistic option on the cards if Germany was to be defeated.

It was not, therefore, one can argue, that French was a bad general so much as a leader utterly ill-prepared and lacking in experience for modern war. Haig, one could suggest, was equally unprepared for the task ahead, a colonial warrior also unfitted for a slow and painful campaign of attrition, as those under his command would now discover.

PART THREE

THE YEAR OF SLAUGHTER

THE BATTLE OF VERDUN

February 21st–December 18th 1916

The ten-month battle or siege of frontier fortresses at Verdun was the most bloodthirsty of all the German/French exchanges throughout the war, with hundreds of thousands dead on each side by its end. The aim of Falkenhayn, the German overall commander, was to batter the French into unacceptable levels of casualties so that they would want to end the war: as he declared, 'the forces of France will bleed to death'.

Ironically, however, the German losses were equally severe, and the bloodbath was to have devastating effects on both sides. Including the carnage further down the Western Front, at the Somme, where tens of thousands of British and Empire soldiers died, the losses overall in 1916 were unimaginably high, and have created the image of World War I that we recall today.

The French had in past times believed in fortresses and, with the building of the Maginot Line after 1918, were to do so again. But Verdun in 1916 was not heavily fortified, as some of the major guns had been sent away for use on the Western Front. Verdun was a place of symbolism, one of the territories granted to France some centuries before in 1648, during the golden age of Bourbon rule. Now its destruction by the Germans would cause France to give up the fight and thus exit the conflict. As historian John Keegan has summarised it, if 'the French gave up the struggle, they would lose Verdun; if they persisted they would lose the war'. They did not lose Verdun, but the casualties would be so high as to feel like a major loss.

Bad weather postponed the original assault, aimed for February 10th. The actual bombardment thus began on February 21st. No fewer than 80,000 German shells pulverised a small area no more than 500 by 1,000 yards square. The attack proved successful, since within three days all the French outer defences at Verdun had been both penetrated and captured. On February 25th one of the outer forts, Douaumont, fell to the Germans.

So many hundreds of thousands of French troops were to die in defending Verdun that some historians have wondered whether or not it would have saved French lives if the city and its fortress had fallen as well. But the French were made of sterner stuff, and, just as the Germans hoped, they decided to put everything into the defence of Verdun. The hideous battle of attrition had begun.

On February 25th General Edouard de Castelnau ordered that as many of the forward positions should be held as possible. The commander put in charge was General Philippe Pétain, who in this fight to the death was to be France's saviour, but who, twenty-four years later, in 1940, would surrender to Germany.

Pétain made two vital strategic assessments. Firstly, supply routes absolutely had to be maintained. Some 12,000 lorries would now brave the battle conditions and trundle down the narrow 'sacred way' to Verdun, bringing, on a daily basis, the supplies the defenders needed simply to survive and to carry on.

With them came shells that enabled the second part of Pétain's plan: a counter-bombardment that would put the Germans under the same level of artillery barrage as the defenders had suffered just a few days before. By February 27th the Germans had reached the point of maximum French resistance. Both sides were now shelling each other mercilessly and with terrifying accuracy.

By April it was obvious to the German commander, Falkenhayn, that his plan of attrition was not working as originally planned. The Germans were now incurring massive losses themselves. From April 9th–13th the French launched an enormous bombardment on a twenty-mile front, only to be halted by another enemy, the torrential rain that effectively postponed further assaults until May.

French tactics and ways of fighting also helped the defence. Pétain realised that soldiers could fight much better if rotated, so that the same troops were not always under the maximum stress in the same place. Some forty-two divisions were therefore rotated through Verdun from other parts of the front. German troops, however, were the same throughout, so the longer the struggle continued the more exhausted they became.

The casualties were now building up to unacceptable levels, so Pétain was moved elsewhere to be replaced by an up-and-coming artillery expert, General Robert Nivelle. With him the French bombardment was to become far more severe.

But even this did not break the resolve of the attackers. In June a further German assault began. On June 7th the fortress of Vaux fell to the invaders. In a rare chivalrous gesture, Crown Prince Wilhelm, the titular German commander, presented the defending French officer, Major Raynal, with a replacement sword. Then on June 22nd a new German attack began, this time also with chlorine gas.

This was, historians agree, the high point of the campaign. German attempts to get further and to capture more fortresses and Verdun itself were beginning to prove futile. July 11th saw one final heave, only for it to fail. Then in October the French counter-attack began, and by

December their forces were almost where they had been before all the fighting had begun back in February.

Hundreds of thousands of German and French troops had been killed – for what? As always, death tolls and statistics are notoriously difficult to agree upon, but it would seem, roughly speaking, that the French lost around 377,000 casualties and the Germans approximately 337,000. That is a possible total of 714,000 people; even given the margin of error, *both* sides suffered from hideous attrition. The Germans had a taste of their own medicine, and the carnage continued into 1917.

The successful defence of Verdun was to become part of French folklore, as indeed it should. The losses were terrible, but at least France had not lost. The effect on morale, however, was detrimental to the Allied cause – as would become clear as the new year began.

THE BATTLE OF THE SOMME

July 1st–November 18th/19th 1916

The Battle of the Somme is one of the best known in the story of warfare. One writer, Correlli Barnett, has called its first day 'a catastrophe without parallel in British history'. The late John Keegan has aptly described the 'holocaust of the Somme' for the United Kingdom and Empire as the 'greatest tragedy of their military history'. Over the weeks in which it was fought, the British and Empire losses came to nearly 420,000 and the French to a little under 195,000 – the main French casualties having been, as we have just seen, at Verdun.

The memory of the Somme has lasted in a way that is true of few of the battles fought by Britain over its long history. Furthermore, it had a huge impact for decades afterwards. When an irate American statesman came to London during the Second World War, to stiffen the sinews, as he saw it, of the casualty-averse British, the response he got from Churchill's personal Chief of Staff, General Ismay, was '60,000 on the first day of the Somme'.

In fact, there were 57,000 casualties, of which 19,000 were deaths and the rest injuries, but with such large numbers who would quibble over a slight exaggeration? And remember – that is the toll of the first day alone. In the case of one regiment, from Newfoundland, ninety per cent of the soldiers were wiped out in the first attack. That kind of carnage is never forgotten.

So, how did it come to this?

Scores of books have been written purely about the Somme itself. But perhaps the best account is to be found in a wider-ranging book on the subject of how the ordinary British soldier survived this battle at all, and those throughout history. This is *The Face of Battle* by John Keegan, who taught military history for many years to soldiers at the Royal Military Academy in Sandhurst: a historian teaching the practitioners.

What made the battle particularly traumatic for the British was the type of men engaged in the fighting. The original army of pre-August 1914 were long-term professional soldiers, but many of those now fighting at the Somme were 'Pals' battalions, people from the same village or factory or trade association, all of whom had volunteered to join together. Consequently, if one particular regiment was obliterated, the impact on the town or village or factory would be especially devastating, since most of the men who lived or worked there would be killed all at once.

So tragically, as Keegan shows us, the devastation of the battlefield was replicated in the soldiers' places of origin back home.

It is also important to note that like was not fighting like, something that we all too easily forget, but which became a key factor for British (and Commonwealth) forces in each of the World Wars. Battles are truly horrific in nature, but the context for the tragedy in nations such as the United Kingdom, Australia, Canada (and the USA for most of its history, for which 'the draft' has been the exception not the rule) is rather different.

Traditional European countries such as France and Germany have always had peace-time conscription, with young men of the right military age being obliged to spend time in the armed services, whether their nation is at war or peace. In Britain this has been very much the exception. The era of conscription without a major war, from 1945–1958, was highly unusual. In 1939 the British government introduced it straight away, but so unusual was it normally that conscription did not come to the United Kingdom in World War I until 1916, two years after the fighting had begun. As the Boer War and the various colonial wars in which a young Winston Churchill was involved all show, the British had not really fought a proper European-wide war since 1815 (if we exclude the Crimean War as a distant exception).

Thus, when World War I began the British had just four infantry divisions in Flanders (and one cavalry). What is so astonishing, and a massive tribute to British skill and ingenuity, is that by July 1st 1916, less than two years later, there were now fifty-eight infantry divisions ready to fight, an increase unparalleled in the country's history. Yet these divisions largely consisted of very poorly trained conscript troops, most of whom had never expected to leave civilian life. The same strictures could surely apply to the commanders themselves. Many of them had Boer War experience, but that was more of a guerrilla campaign than the trench-based war of attrition that was now taking place in France and Flanders. Being an officer of a professional army in a colonial war is a very different matter from commanding conscripts – essentially civilians in uniform – in a European theatre of war against a highly trained enemy. Germany and France, meanwhile, had possessed conscripted armies for years, and on an altogether more gigantic scale. This meant that there were numerous German officers already trained to lead large numbers of men, something not at all the case with Britain.

As well as the nature of the British troops, many

have attributed blame for the disaster of the Somme to Sir Douglas Haig. Few generals have proved as deeply controversial and it is his decisions on the Somme that have created the main debate on his effectiveness. Haig was lambasted posthumously by Britain's great political leader David Lloyd George (who was Secretary of State for War during the Somme, following Kitchener's death at sea, and Prime Minister from December 1916 to 1922). Since that time many soldiers and some civilian writers, such as his former aide General Sir James Marshall-Cornwall and the historian John Terraine, have tried to rehabilitate his reputation. Indeed, it is the current trend to do so.

But what these biographers do is to look at the massive victories of 1918, when Haig was still in command (to Lloyd George's despair) and read his successes backwards. If Haig was so triumphant in 1918, they argue, he cannot have been that bad in 1916 and 1917. This approach is perhaps a mistake, and so perhaps it is valid to examine the decisions taken by those such as Haig.

Soldiers understandably do not like 'armchair generals' who refight old battles – always with hindsight – and show how victory could have been won, or at least achieved at far lower human cost. But all history involves consideration of *why* things happened rather than just a boring narrative of *what* took place. In the case of the Battle of the Somme even historians who have served in real battles themselves can see how things could have turned out very differently from the way in which they did. To lose 420,000 soldiers in just a few weeks merits some examination.

The battle was fought in one of the areas most strongly defended by the German army, some of whose bunkers were thirty feet deep and thus impervious to bombardment by even the best available Allied artillery. The reason for the venue is that it was the part of the front closest to the French position. Thus placing troops there would be of inestimable help to the latter's heavily besieged armies at Verdun. It is important to note that Haig would have wanted the soldiers under his command to attack German positions anyway, but that a purely British and Empire attack would have taken place both later in the year and possibly at a more auspicious part of the front. Nevertheless the principle of attack was as much Haig's as that of the desperate French, contrary to legend.

British artillery was nowhere near as good in 1916 as it was to be in 1918, when the skills necessary to launch a bombardment were to become more accurate. Also shells that were technically far superior would be acquired. Far too many of those fired in 1916 were duds, or incapable of destroying trenches as deep as those dug by the Germans. And while the 'Pals Brigades' had plenty of camaraderie, they were, in terms of fighting prowess, nowhere near as skilled or well trained as their German opponents.

Sir Henry Rawlinson, the British Fourth Army commander, was a proponent of what was called 'bite and hold': a limited advance, with concentrated heavy bombardment, to an achievable goal, and consolidation of that gain before going on to the next objective. In an army in which many of the senior commanders were former cavalrymen, it is significant that Rawlinson was an infantryman by training, and someone who had studied the tactics of armies in other wars, such as the Russo-Japanese War of 1905. Since it was the Fourth Army during the Somme that suffered by far the most casualties, however, it is understandable that Rawlinson emerged from the final battle with what his biographers have called 'a mixed record'.

Haig on the other hand wanted a broad-front attack, with the bombardment stretching the full length of the front. He even had unrealistic hopes that the war could be won via the Somme, and Rawlinson's caution that it was better to achieve realistic goals – such as one German line at a time – was overruled.

When the assault began on July 1st, all Rawlinson's fears were proved correct – not that he knew that at the time, since the hideous death toll on that day took a while to filter through. It proved almost impossible to cut through the German barbed wire. As a result, when the British and Empire troops were told to *walk* across No Man's Land to maintain cohesion, thousands of them were mowed down by the well-entrenched and defended German machine-gunners with the greatest of ease.

Rawlinson has been blamed as the man in direct charge, and Haig as the overall general whose orders set the tone. In retrospect it would seem that Rawlinson's caution might have saved thousands of lives, but given the lack of technical and tactical edge that the Allies possessed, the death toll at the Somme would surely have been hideous either way.

What is inexcusable, and with Haig as the senior commander, is that Haig continued to try to push against the German positions long after it became evident that the attack was going nowhere. Even the advent of a few early prototype tanks in a second offensive, on September 15th, made barely any difference. Many of the tanks simply broke down. Not until November was the overall attack called off, with well over 400,000 British and Empire casualties, and with no real victory to justify such an exceptional loss of life.

Yet come 1918, Rawlinson's 'bite and hold' proved to be a winner, and troops under Haig's command swept to victory, including at the Somme. There were the same leaders, the same place, but an altogether different outcome and with much smaller losses.

Writers have commented that there was no Napoleon or Wellington in the First World War, and that is certainly true of the attrition and carnage on the Western Front. No great leader emerged, though one could make a case that eventually in Marshal Foch of France the Allies had a supreme commander with the tactical grip of an Eisenhower. But while the commanders were the same, the circumstances of 1918 were to be very different, as we shall discover.

But first there was the further carnage of 1917, the near collapse of the French army in mutiny, and the disintegration of Russia in revolution and civil war. The Allies still had a long way to go and much suffering to endure.

THE BATTLE OF JUTLAND

May 31st–June 1st 1916

Winston Churchill once said of Admiral Sir John Jellicoe that he was the only man who could lose the war in an afternoon. When war broke out in 1914, Jellicoe was promoted to Commander-in-Chief of the Home Fleet. In effect this was the part of the Royal Navy that was responsible for the protection of the United Kingdom against the Germans and for ensuring that Britain, an island nation, could not be starved into submission. (The official name for the Royal Navy force and for those Canadian and Australian ships fighting with them is the 'Grand Fleet', while their German opponents were the 'High Seas Fleet'.)

Historically Britain had always been a primarily naval power. The Royal Navy was at the core of British tradition and defence. This is why the British Expeditionary Force in both 1914 and again in 1939 were each so small. It was simply not the tradition to have what is called a 'continental commitment', a large land army for use in fighting on European soil. There was a large army in India, but even there most of the ordinary soldiers were Indian and it was only the officer class that was principally British.

The events of 1914–1916 soon saw the United Kingdom having to create an army from scratch. It is a considerable tribute to those who achieved mass mobilisation – without conscription until 1916 – that the British Expeditionary Force was able to grow as fast and effectively as it did.

The Royal Navy, however, was different. Historian Correlli Barnett, an expert on how Britain has often lagged behind on using technological change, has made the following observation: by the time we reached 1914 and an actual European war, the Royal Navy was not the fine victory-winning force that it had been in its glory days of Admiral Nelson, the Battle of Trafalgar and the Napoleonic Wars.

This is not to say that the Royal Navy had not done its best to catch up with some of the latest technological developments. This was especially true under its political overlord Winston Churchill, who served as First Lord of the Admiralty with much enthusiasm from 1911–1915.

In fact, the early twentieth century saw a major arms race in naval construction between Britain and its rival

Germany. Both powers sought to develop a dynamic and wholly new class of battleship, the dreadnought, which was technologically in advance of its predecessors. The United Kingdom and Germany found themselves locked in competition, each nation attempting to construct more of these naval behemoths than the other.

Not only was this very expensive, but it also, historians have argued, made any attempts at German-British reconciliation during the Edwardian period far more difficult. Nationalist sentiment was easily stirred up in both countries as the race progressed, with, for example, British patriotic cries of 'we want eight and we won't wait' as the demand to build ever more dreadnoughts continued.

But even in naval matters Britain, while ahead in the construction race, was not fully up to par with all the latest technology. British battleships still did not have the night-time firing capacity that their German equivalents possessed, nor were their hulls as strongly armour-plated. Therefore the British were still left with major vulnerabilities should their ships ever be attacked.

In December 1914 the Royal Navy had been able to sink four major German battleships in an engagement in the Falkland Islands, thousands of miles away from home. In exchange for twenty-five injured Royal Navy sailors, no fewer than 2,200 Germans died. The fifth German ship escaped, but had sustained such great damage that it could not be saved, so in March 1915 it was destroyed. In the skirmish known as the Battle of the Dogger Bank (in the North Sea) in January 1915 several German major ships were damaged or sunk, with far fewer British losses.

Consequently, although the High Seas Fleet had, in theory, some of the very finest ships in the world, the Germans decided to keep their navy in harbour, away from possible danger. Only in East Asia, with the victories of the German battleship *Emden* in the Indian Ocean, were they to have any success against the Royal Navy.

However, in January 1916, a new commander was appointed to lead the High Seas Fleet: Vice-Admiral Reinhard Scheer. He felt ashamed at the timidity of his country, and was determined to give the Grand Fleet as much trouble as possible. He therefore began some daring raids, designed to provoke the British into action. Some of his ships sailed provocatively near the Dogger Bank, and German Zeppelin airships raided the English east coast.

Then on May 30th 1916 the High Seas Fleet finally emerged from their harbour, with the aim of setting a trap for the Grand Fleet off the western coast of Denmark, or Jutland. This was a clever move; Germany had the smaller fleet but hoped to destroy part of the more powerful British fleet by luring them into a direct engagement. The long-awaited conflict between the two navies had finally begun.

Here we can divert to a salutary lesson. Breaking the enemy codes can save lives and shorten a war. But if the right intercept does not get to the correct person in time, then it does no good, as Britain was to discover in both world wars. The Admiralty code-breakers, nicknamed 'Room 40' after their location in the Admiralty, had enjoyed some success in cracking some German naval codes. In 1916 Jellicoe knew from the Room 40 intercepts that Scheer and the High Seas Fleet had sailed. But what he did not know was precisely where the Germans were because of a failure in communication.

Not only that, but as Correlli Barnett and other historians have pointed out, Jellicoe was in effect still dependent on much eighteenth-century technology. This was the age before radar, and naval commanders had to rely on lookouts at the tops of masts, and on signalling other ships by flag. This was not how to fight a twentieth-century war! And as Barnett adds, the rigidity of the hierarchy within the Royal Navy suppressed the kind of dash and individual initiative that had made Nelson so great in Napoleonic times. The Grand Fleet was very much under Jellicoe's command and would act only when he gave the orders.

When the fleets engaged on May 31st, there were 99 ships in the High Seas Fleet, 16 of which were dreadnought class. The Grand Fleet possessed 151 ships, many of which were quite old, but with 28 dreadnought-class vessels. Jellicoe was in overall charge of the latter, with the younger Admiral Sir David Beatty in command of those ships expecting to find and sink the Germans.

What happened next is quite confusing, and has been hotly debated by historians and sailors ever since. Within a few minutes of the first exchange of fire, Beatty's own flagship was damaged and several British ships either sunk or badly hit. German losses were smaller but Beatty, in the Nelson tradition, commanded his ships to 'engage the enemy closer'.

After further fighting, which books on the Battle of Jutland explain in considerable detail, Beatty's ships saw that the main fleet under Jellicoe was in sight – and that Scheer's principal force was a mere twelve miles ahead. So Beatty now ordered his part of the British fleet to steer towards Jellicoe's approaching ships in order, as Correlli Barnett puts it, to act as bait for the Germans. But this meant that the forward part of the Grand Fleet put itself into the full range of the German High Seas Fleet. The British flagship was sunk, with its commander Admiral Sir Horace Hood drowning with his ship. Other Royal Navy cruisers were also destroyed.

But now Jellicoe and the main part of the Grand Fleet had arrived, putting themselves into what is called the T position, the Germans being the vertical stroke and the British the horizontal. This was a famous old navy manoeuvre that Jellicoe hoped would do the trick. Scheer, however, managed to get his ships to turn 180 degrees, thus escaping most of the British gunfire. But he deceived himself, since, in the belief that he had successfully achieved his goal, he then ordered his fleet to turn 180 degrees again. This put them back into British fire and many German ships were sunk or damaged.

However, Jellicoe now possibly snatched an unambiguous victory from the Royal Navy. Terrified of torpedo attacks upon his ships, he ordered the Grand Fleet to turn back. All was not totally lost, though. Scheer had lost several ships in what is termed a 'death ride' attack on the Royal Navy, while some of his other ships had managed to survive through the manoeuvre. So he tried to escape with as much of his fleet as he could, taking full advantage of the fact that British ships were not able to fight as well at night as their German equivalents.

The High Seas Fleet thus managed to get back to port. But were they safe home to fight another day?

Technically speaking there is or should be no doubt that Jutland was a German victory. Jellicoe and Beatty between them had lost three battle cruisers, three ordinary cruisers, eight destroyers and 6,274 officers and shipmen, and all in a single night. By contrast, Scheer had lost just one battleship, one battle cruiser, four light cruisers and five destroyers, with the lower death toll of 2,524 officers and shipmen.

However, the High Seas Fleet never again left port. They contemplated a brief foray on August 18th only to return quickly. Apart from a few minor skirmishes with limited numbers of vessels, nothing major ever happened again.

The vast investment Britain and Germany had poured into the naval arms race before 1914 was now for nothing, since the two fleets were never to engage again. For the most part all the German effort had been useless, since in effect Britannia still ruled the waves, remaining in control of the North Sea.

So who actually won Jutland? The outcome of the largest naval battle of WWI was indecisive. We can perhaps leave the last word with an American journalist who wrote at the time: 'The German Fleet has assaulted its jailer; but it is still in jail.'

THE BRUSILOV OFFENSIVE

June 4th–September 20th 1916

It is easy to forget, especially in reading about different fronts during a conflict, that events on one front can profoundly affect those on another, even hundreds of miles away.

The great bloodletting on the Western Front in 1916 – at Verdun and the Somme – meant that the Russians wanted to do all that was possible to help their British and French allies. Russia, in turn, was aided by the presence of Italian forces fighting against Austria-Hungary on the Isonzo River plains that year. As it turned out, this proved to be a military disaster for Italy. Nonetheless, the fact that the Austrians were obliged to move troops from the Carpathians to Italy was a boon for the Russians.

So although the battles fought on the Eastern Front were a long way from both northern Italy and from the French/Belgian border, all the campaigns in 1916 were interlinked.

The French needed a major German diversion from Verdun, and so the Russians decided in March to come to their aid. They launched a campaign near Lake Naroch, close to the town then called Vilna (now the Lithuanian city of Vilnius). But what should have been a major breakthrough because of considerable Russian superiority in troop numbers turned out to be a disaster. Between March 18th and 31st they lost over 100,000 men, including 12,000 to exposure in the savage winter conditions. Many of those killed were victims of 'friendly fire'. No fewer than 15,000 soldiers died in the first eight hours on March 4th. In April the Germans, who had lost only a fifth of the number of Russian casualties, were able to take back the tiny amount of ground that they had lost. It was not looking promising for the Allies, with the Russians suffering so many deaths, and countless injuries being inflicted on the Western Front.

In the summer of 1916 General Aleksei Brusilov, one of the younger up-and-coming Russian generals, realised that he had a major opportunity to inflict massive damage on Germany's weaker ally, the Austrians. However, whereas the Russian armies fighting the Germans had larger and theoretically more powerful forces, on the southern (Russian/Austrian) front, the two armies were evenly matched in size. Brusilov decided that he would attack on as wide a front as possible, making it difficult for the Austrians to concentrate their defences at any one particular strong point.

His offensive began on June 4th, and it was successful from the beginning. Aerial photography played a key role in finding out where his enemy was entrenched. In the south, in the Carpathians, the Austrian Seventh Army was rent asunder, and rapidly lost over 100,000 soldiers, many of them as prisoners of war. Many Czech soldiers, with decreasing loyalty to the Habsburg dynasty, simply surrendered en masse. By the middle of that month the Austro-Hungarian armies were in retreat everywhere. Brusilov had managed to gain a foothold in hitherto Austrian-held territory twenty kilometres wide and seventy-five kilometres deep. In order to help their beleaguered ally, the Germans had been obliged to transfer divisions from Verdun, where they had been urgently needed, to the Carpathian front, where they were necessary to prevent an Austrian disaster.

By September Brusilov's campaign was overwhelmingly victorious. He had by now taken over 400,000 as prisoners of war, and inflicted losses of over 600,000 men. Even though his colleagues fighting against the Germans had not quite the same degree of military success, they had inflicted 350,000 casualties on the

German army, and managed to advance an astonishing sixty miles into enemy territory. No Western army had ever come even remotely that close to capturing German occupied areas.

Sadly the offensive now ran out of steam. The transport logistics simply did not allow for the Russians to get any further and this meant that the troops were now too far ahead of their supply base. By September 15th the increased number of German divisions was also making a difference to Brusilov's colleagues since the former were an altogether stronger foe.

By September 20th the offensive was over. But despite hideous casualties – perhaps as many as a million captured, wounded or killed – the Russian achievement was nonetheless astonishing. Half the Austro-Hungarian army had been destroyed, and it has been argued that the German transfer of troops was the key event that saved Verdun.

Historian David Stevenson has called it the 'biggest Allied success since the Marne' in 1914 when Joffre was able to halt what had seemed to be an inevitable defeat. John Keegan has written that the 'Brusilov offensive was, on the scale by which success was measured in the foot-by-foot fighting of the First World War, the greatest victory seen on any front since the trench lines had been dug on the Aisne two years before'.

Brusilov was perhaps therefore the most successful

Allied general of the whole war, yet he is virtually unknown and unheralded in the West. Many have heard of Zhukov in the Second World War, yet Brusilov is an unfamiliar name. He was to be one of the few tsarist generals to make peace with the Bolsheviks after 1917, and to die peacefully in his bed.

THE BATTLE OF ARRAS AND
THE NIVELLE OFFENSIVE

Spring 1917

After the two slaughterhouses of the Somme for the British and Verdun for the French, these two key Allies were determined that never again should such carnage take place. But if we think back to the very valid comments made of Neuve-Chapelle on the functional and structural issues that no side addressed adequately, we realise that these vital problems remained unresolved. Sadly nothing was going to change in late 1916, however much the Allied leadership might have wished otherwise.

The new and dynamic British leader David Lloyd George became Prime Minister in December 1916. He had been a successful Minister of Munitions, doing his best to reduce the terrible shortage of shells and equipment for the BEF. After Kitchener's death at sea he served briefly as Secretary of State for War, before deposing his lacklustre predecessor as Prime Minister in a virtual political coup with Conservative support.

Lloyd George was horrified by the needless death toll on the Western Front, and did not rate Haig highly – he was to eviscerate the general in his later memoirs of the war. But since his government was dependent on Conservative support, and because Haig also had a direct line of communication to King George V, Lloyd George was circumscribed in what he could do to change the military command. This was so unlike Churchill in World War II, whose more secure political base meant that he could sack and promote generals almost at will.

Lloyd George was a passionate 'Easterner', something that would soon make a major difference to the war in the Middle East. But in Europe he was stuck with Haig. Soon, however, a major shift in French opinion came to his rescue. In December 1916 Joffre, unpopular since the horrors of Verdun, was dropped, in favour of a dynamic new commander, General Robert Nivelle. The latter was a man with a mission, convinced that he possessed the secret that had hitherto eluded all others on how finally to break through German lines and win the war. As historian Correlli Barnett puts it so well, the French government now put its faith in this new leader 'as a sick man puts his faith in the miracle cure of a quack'.

Since Nivelle was half-English he could communicate easily with the British and thereby won over Lloyd George as well, especially since it would be French troops engaged in the main offensive rather than the BEF under Haig. However, when Lloyd George consequently asked for Haig's forces to be under Nivelle's command, the British military reacted ferociously, to an extent to which Britain's civilian leadership never subsequently regained the trust of the Armed Forces during the rest of the war. This was, naturally, not helpful.

Nivelle postponed all thought of offensive action from February, when it had been originally planned, to April. This gave plenty of breathing space to the Germans to rearrange their positions. But the space also proved useful retrenching time for French commanders such as Pétain, the hero of Verdun, for whom Nivelle's schemes were ludicrous.

Thus in April two offensives took place: the British (and Empire troops) at Arras, and the French along the River Aisne.

The British bombardment began on April 9th. The Canadians were able to score a notable success at Vimy Ridge from April 9th to 12th, under their commander General Julian Byng. Although the rest of the battle front was not as successful, historian John Keegan has noted that the 'first day of the Battle of Arras was a British triumph'. Hopes that this would be the longed-for breakthrough were thus high.

However, France's own attack, launched a week later on April 16th, was to prove a disaster. Nivelle believed in what he called 'rupture' or a major break in enemy lines. The problem was that it was the French lines that were ruptured, and not the Germans'. Bombardment had given the game away and the German guns were ready for them. Centring around Chemin des Dames, the battle began with much expectation. But the French failed utterly to co-ordinate their artillery barrage with their troop movements, with the result that thousands of their soldiers were mown down by accurate German machine-gun fire.

In 1918 the deployment of tanks would make a huge difference to Western victory. But the simple possession of tanks in and of themselves was useless if they were not operated properly. In this instance the German artillery was able to destroy the French tanks while they were still in column formation and before they could be launched effectively from the trenches.

The French position soon collapsed into a fiasco. Some 29,000 troops were killed and overall some 120,000 were dead, wounded or captured. Not surprisingly Nivelle's command did not survive this disaster, and he was sacked on May 15th, to be replaced by Pétain, the hero of Verdun.

The British kept going valiantly until May 16th, when they had to stop. Australian forces had fought well, and despite the fact that there were some 158,000 casualties overall among British and Empire forces, this was no repeat of the carnage of the Somme.

Significantly, morale among British and Empire forces remained intact. This was not the case at all with the French. A major mutiny broke out on April 29th and although it was not violent, it had a dreadful effect on France's war effort. Pétain was asked to suppress it, which he did with tact.

What had begun as the hope of victory had ended in disaster. The fighting would continue. But now the Americans were on their way . . .

PART FOUR

A YEAR OF REVOLUTIONS
The Russian Revolutions and the USA enters the war.

AMERICA ENTERS THE WAR

April 1917

In March 1917 Germany announced unrestricted submarine warfare against ships supplying their enemies, thus bringing the USA reluctantly into the war. Strictly speaking this decision was not based upon a single event or a particular battle, although German torpedoes had sunk several US ships. What were the factors that led Germany to this decision?

The idea of letting U-boat commanders sink whatever they wished was the decision of Admiral Henning von Holtzendorff, the Chief of Staff of the German Navy. He had calculated that if hundreds of thousands of tons worth of British shipping were sunk each month, the United Kingdom would be starved into submission, possibly as soon as within five months of the campaign being launched.

Royal Navy ships were themselves carrying out a great job in restricting trade that could reach Germany. In the end it would be the Germans who were starved, first into surrender in 1918 and then, in 1919, into signing the Treaty of Versailles, since the Allied blockade continued beyond the end of the war. So the policy backfired, as it was Germany's enemy that succeeded in implementing it.

The decision to attack US ships also proved to be very foolish. While attacks in the Mediterranean and off the French coast against *British* vessels were all part of the existing conflict, attacks on *American* vessels, those of an officially neutral nation, were another matter altogether.

President Woodrow Wilson had won the presidential election in 1916 partly on a platform of keeping the USA out of conflicts in the Old World. He felt that America was 'too proud to fight'.

We now think of the USA as being inevitably and inextricably involved in global affairs. This has certainly been the case since the decision, taken by President Truman in the 1940s, to keep US forces permanently overseas, and to be involved in projects such as the Marshall Plan, or organisations such as the UN and NATO.

Historically, however, things were very different indeed. In essence, the nineteenth-century non-interference Monroe Doctrine of 1823, enunciated by US President James Monroe, promoted self-rule for the Americas, insisting that Old World powers in Europe should keep out of the internal affairs of the American hemisphere. The unspoken corollary was that America would in effect do the same in reverse – keep well out of European affairs and conflicts. After all, the very nature of the American idea was to have a country for people who wanted to leave the Old World behind and create a New World far from their home countries. Wilson therefore was, in 1916, sticking firmly to the original US script.

But then on March 15th 1917, fifteen German U-boats directly attacked American merchant ships, sinking three of them. This was an outrage to the USA, having the kind of psychological effect that was seen at Pearl Harbour in 1941 and on 9/11 in 2001. The USA had wanted to keep away from Old World conflicts, but now the Germans had foolishly brought the war to America.

The other main cause for US entry into the war was what is called the 'Zimmermann telegram'. Henry Stimson, a distinguished American politician who served in the US government in the 1920s and 1930s and again during World War II, is notoriously alleged to have said 'Gentlemen do not read each other's mail'. It is as well that the British government thought otherwise, since they were doing everything possible to break as many German codes as they could, famously in Room 40 in the Admiralty. In 1917 they came across a telegram sent by Arthur Zimmermann, the new German Foreign Minister, dated January 16th and addressed to his Ambassador in Washington DC, Count Bernstorff, for forwarding to the German Embassy in Mexico City.

During 1914–1915, there had been small wars between the USA and Mexico over who should rule the latter country. Mexico's northern neighbour was flagrantly interfering in its internal affairs. Yet this was entirely compatible with the Monroe Doctrine. The USA gave itself the right to look after affairs in its own backyard. America had looked very askance when European powers, led by Emperor Napoleon III of France, had briefly attempted to impose a Habsburg Archduke as Emperor of Mexico back in the mid-nineteenth century.

This hostility between the US and Mexico was something that the Germans felt that they could exploit. Zimmermann, in his telegram, therefore offered to Mexico the territories that it had lost to the USA in the 1840s, including Texas, New Mexico and Arizona. In return Mexico would join Germany at war against the USA.

Germany was in effect both declaring war on the USA and then flagrantly breaking the Monroe Doctrine by seeking direct involvement in the internal affairs of the Western hemisphere. American troops had only just left Mexico, in January–February 1917, and now here was Germany seeking to come to that country's aid at the expense of the USA.

It seems that Wilson himself discovered the contents

of the telegram on February 24th, via a note from Arthur Balfour, the British Foreign Secretary, in audience with the US Ambassador in London. But what arguably tipped the scales completely was the publication of the telegram to the US general public on March 1st. As writers have noted, not even the sinking of the *Lusitania* in 1915, with the loss of many innocent American lives, had persuaded the still-isolationist government and ordinary citizen of the need to be involved in the war. The Zimmermann telegram provoked a response of vast outrage on a national scale.

It was an exceedingly risky thing to do – countries do not normally reveal that they have broken the secret codes and cyphers of their enemies: the Enigma/ULTRA secret of World War II remained just that for over thirty years. But the risk now was clearly worth it, as events went on to show.

So now there was both the Zimmermann telegram and the sinking of American merchant ships by U-boats, both in breach of US neutrality. While Irish Americans, many of whom hated Britain, and German Americans, loyal to the country of their ancestors, were reluctant to be involved, the mass of public opinion swelled up behind the President, creating a political momentum that not even the most isolationist politician in the Senate or the House of Representatives could gainsay.

By March 21st Wilson had decided for war. He spelt it out to Congress on April 2nd, paraphrasing at the end

the words of sixteenth-century Martin Luther in defiance
before the Holy Roman Emperor at the Diet of Worms:

> To such a task we can dedicate our lives and our
> fortunes, everything that we are and everything we
> have, with the pride of those who know that the day
> has come when America is privileged to spend her
> blood and her might for the principles that gave her
> birth and happiness and the peace which she has
> treasured. God helping her, she can do no other.

On April 6th 1917 came the declaration of war itself,
with Wilson promising to use 'force to the uttermost,
force without stint or limit'. As we shall see in another
chapter, it took a while for the full force of the USA to
be felt, especially in terms of troop numbers shipped to
Europe to fight alongside Britain and France. But when
the Americans did come, they arrived in their hundreds of
thousands, a fresh and dynamic replacement force that the
Central Powers could not even remotely begin to match.
Theoretically speaking, the USA was only an Associate
Power, declaring war later on other Central Powers, but in
practice the US was rapidly becoming the superpower we
know it as today.

There were now 93.4 million American citizens on the
side of the British and French Empires against Germany
and the Central Powers. The annual steel production

of the USA was three times that of both Germany and Austria-Hungary put together. The US Navy was second in size only to that of Britain. New technology meant that the U-boat threat diminished as the war now progressed, so that no US soldiers were to lose their lives crossing the Atlantic to fight in France. By 1918 the increasing use of the new device of naval convoys by the British Admiralty had greatly reduced German submarine power. The balance of the war had been irreversibly changed, though it would take over another year for the full impact to be felt.

While the entry of the USA was the key event of 1917, some other battles took place, along with the revolutions in Russia. We will consider these in the chapters that follow.

RETAKING KUT AND CAPTURING BAGHDAD

February–March 1917

After the disgrace at Kut in 1915, the British were naturally very wary of launching an army only to face another utter disaster in the desert. The new British general in charge, Sir Stanley Maude, was thus highly cautious. While his troops were under the command of the War Office in London, most of them were part of the Indian army, and they arrived slowly but surely by sea to Basra, the port at the top of the Persian Gulf, towards the end of 1916.

Most of the Turkish/Ottoman casualties during this time had been on the front against the Russians. The previous year, in 1915, these deaths had led to one of the greatest tragedies not just of the First World War but of any conflict: the massacre of possibly as many as a million Armenians by the Ottoman forces. Some of Armenia was in the Russian Empire (where the country of that name is today) but at that time a large proportion of the Armenian population lived in present-day Turkey. Since the Ottomans did not trust the loyalty of the Armenians, who shared the Christian faith of Russia, millions of innocent men, women and children were forcibly evacuated and countless numbers died. Even today the Turkish government still tries to deny that the Armenian massacres ever took place. The Armenian diaspora in California and elsewhere has not ceased to make these horrors as great an issue as the Jewish Holocaust later in the century.

By 1916 the Russo-Turkish war was still in full spate, which meant that reinforcement of the southern frontier of the Ottoman Empire was going to be difficult to achieve. As a result, 150,000 British-led troops were able to land without hindrance in the port of Basra, ready to avenge the defeat and humiliation of Kut. Remember one thing: at that time the whole area simply consisted of provinces of the far larger Ottoman Empire. British forces were again to be based in Basra after 2003, but in a country we now call Iraq. Back then no such place existed; what Maude and his troops were able to achieve was to transform the area in a way that they could not themselves have expected when they tentatively set off from Basra in December 1916.

General Maude had learnt the lessons of Townshend's

arrogance and foolishness. He proceeded carefully along both banks of the River Tigris, and never extended beyond his supply base or lines of communication. Townshend had employed, for example, a mere six steamers and eight tugs. Maude now used 446 steam launches and tugs, 414 motor boats and a huge array of no fewer than 774 barges. The contrast could not be greater, nor could the outcome.

By February 24th they had arrived at Kut and this time were able both to take and to hold the town without any difficulty. Then, just over two weeks later, Maude's forces were able to reach Baghdad itself. After a short struggle many of the defenders fled, and the ancient capital of some of the greatest Islamic empires in history, the city of *1001 Nights*, was captured with much ease on March 11th 1917. Maude had lost hardly any troops to death, injury or dehydration.

The Proclamation of Baghdad by Maude announced that 'Our armies do not come into your cities and lands as conquerors or enemies, but as liberators'. Britain now in effect annexed the areas that they had conquered, the Ottoman provinces (named *vilayets*) of Basra and of Baghdad. But the legitimacy of this conquest was not recognised until after the war by the fledgling League of Nations. This new organisation announced in 1921 the existence of a system of *mandates* – in other words, official permission for a victorious power to rule the colonies of defeated empires in the League's name. (The same system continued with the United Nations after World War II.) But in 1917 the British were in possession, and so they decided to stay.

Sir Stanley Maude died, probably of cholera, in November 1917. His successor as de facto ruler of the region and as commander of the British troops was General Sir William Marshall. Under him the army attacked further north in October 1918, capturing the key oil town of Mosul on October 30th. This was the same day that the Ottomans surrendered to Allied forces in the Armistice of Mudros.

Britain now possessed another old Ottoman province, that of Mosul. Under a controversial agreement made with the French and Russians, this part of the old Ottoman Empire was destined to go to France and become part of what we now know as Syria. However, it was British troops who had captured Mosul. The Prime Minister David Lloyd George discovered that there was considerable potential for the discovery of oil in that former province. He was, therefore, over the next three years, able to persuade the French into giving it up.

The country we now call Iraq was the creation of Winston Churchill while taking part in a 1921 conference in the Egyptian capital of Cairo. No Arab was present. The two provinces of Basra and Baghdad had been referred to historically as Mesopotamia (the land between the two rivers, the Tigris and the Euphrates), a term that goes back as far as biblical times. But adding the third region, Mosul, created something entirely new that had never before existed. Iraq was an entirely British invention.

The creation of Iraq was possible because of Maude and his brave, successful troops who fought with almost no casualties between December 1916 and October 1918. Without them it is very unlikely that Iraq as we know it in modern times would exist, and the events of the past few decades would have been profoundly different. Once again the achievement of a small number of soldiers back in the First World War changed the world we live in today.

THE BATTLE OF PASSCHENDAELE

July 31st–November 10th 1917

Passchendaele, or the Third Battle of Ypres, was the last of the major battles of attrition of the First World War. Fought between June and November 1917, it cost something over half a million casualties (as usual, exact figures conflict). David Stevenson has described it as 'a wasteful failure'. Hundreds of thousands of brave British, Canadian and other Allied troops were hurled against entrenched German positions, and as at the Battle of the Somme, really to no purpose. As Stevenson laments, 'doing something may be worse than doing nothing', and Passchendaele proved an all too horrible example of just that.

Yet, with the exception of the unlamented General Gough, whose failures ended his career, the commanders in charge of the British and Empire forces at Third Ypres were exactly the same as those who led the Allies to a glorious victory over the Germans in 1918, capturing the huge swathes of territory that had eluded them for the previous four years, and at so devastating a cost in lives.

The series of battles that we name Passchendaele was, according to John Keegan, the 'most notorious land campaign of the war'. It was an entirely British (and Empire) initiative, fought in essence by the BEF on its own. The French mutinies had temporarily rendered that country a difficult ally. (The infant French air force, however, had not mutinied, and so was able to give considerable help to the fledgling Royal Flying Corps in the battles that now followed.)

Haig was all enthusiasm, but the politicians, as before, were highly doubtful. Then a surprise victory, by General Sir Herbert Plumer's Second Army, at Messines Ridge on June 7th provided the catalyst, and the excuse that Haig needed to command an overall assault against the German positions.

The work of the underground miners, digging vast tunnels right underneath enemy lines, has now become famous through television documentaries on these hitherto unknown heroes of the Western Front. At Messines they were exceptionally successful, blowing nineteen mines. Nine divisions moved forward and BEF soldiers found themselves actually able to take German territory, thereby displacing the enemy from the southern section of the Ypres salient. Some 17,000 British and Empire troops were killed or wounded, with over 24,000 German casualties. The fact that this was seen as good news shows how immune to the death toll everyone was becoming.

Politicians were now becoming aware of the replacement issue. With the numbers of casualties so massive, finding able-bodied replacements back home was becoming an increasing problem. Death was not only tragic; the soldiers lost were also irreplaceable. In the chapter on the end of the war we will see how this problem was solved for the Allies by the arrival of hundreds of thousands of Americans, a replacement factor that the Germans simply could not match. But for now the arrival of US troops was in the future and their effect unknown. If too many died, then the army simply could not find substitutes to fill the gaps that the slaughter was creating.

In the Second World War both soldiers and politicians alike were acutely aware of this, but in 1917 Haig seemed to have other ideas: 'it was necessary for us to go on engaging the enemy', he declared. The attrition simply had to continue. And as usual he was wildly optimistic in how far an attack could go.

Unwisely Haig wanted to attack one of the most securely defended parts of the German line, the 'Flanders Position'. Over four million shells rained down upon the Germans in two weeks of heavy bombardment. Then on July 31st at 3 a.m., the BEF advance began. Unfortunately the Germans were able to launch a counter-attack the same day, with a bombardment of their own.

Then came what in many ways was the worst torrent of all – the rain. Three unrelenting days of downpour stopped attackers and defenders alike. As one British commander noted despondently, the mud created chaos: 'The ground is churned up to a depth of ten feet and is the consistency of porridge.' The official history lamented that the earth was 'so slippery from the rain and so broken by the water-filled shell holes that the pace was slow and the protection of the creeping barrage was lost'. Many soldiers simply drowned.

The politicians were appalled at what they saw as an increasingly unnecessary loss of life. Haig has his defenders, both then and now, but his absolute insistence when summoned back to London on September 4th that the attack had to continue surely beggars belief.

It was now up to one of the more competent generals to make what he could of the campaign. Like Sir Henry Rawlinson, mentioned in the chapter on the Battle of the Somme, General Plumer had a policy of 'step-by-step' advance. This involved a period of intense bombardment followed by a realistic level of advance, what he nicknamed 'bite and hold'. In two battles, Polygon Wood on September 26th and Broodseinde on October 4th, his tactics paid off. Ground was captured, and the Germans had to retreat.

Many Australians had fought bravely at Polygon Wood. More ANZAC forces were ordered to capture the village of Passchendaele itself, only for thousands of them to die in a forlorn effort. Now Haig asked the Canadians under his command to continue the process. Unsurprisingly their commander, Sir Arthur Currie, was unwilling to see his troops slaughtered and lost in a similar way. Unlike the poor ANZACs, they were finally able to capture Passchendaele by November 20th, but at the horrific cost of nearly 16,000 killed or wounded. The village itself, as historian Correlli Barnett has observed, was 'no more than a brick-coloured smear in the welter of cratered mud'.

So was any of this vast slaughter necessary? There is huge dispute on the final death toll, but one can safely say that hundreds of thousands of troops died on both sides. Two famous war poets witnessed it, Wilfred Owen and Siegfried Sassoon. What did they think of the value of all this bloodshed and suffering?

Owen called the battlefields in which they died a 'sad land . . . cratered like the moon with hollow woe'. He is particularly expressive about one of the greatest horrors of the Western Front, the use of poison gas. His poem *Dulce et Decorum Est* puts this across in a uniquely vivid way:

Gas! Gas! Quick, boys! – An ecstasy of fumbling,
Fitting the clumsy helmets just in time;
But someone still was yelling out and stumbling,
And flound'ring like a man in fire or lime . . .
Dim, through the misty panes and thick green light,
As under a green sea, I saw him drowning.

Siegfried Sassoon, known for his bravery and recipient of the military cross, reveals his own experience in verse. His poem soon symbolised the feelings of all the participants:

I died in hell
(They called it Passchendaele) my wound was slight
And I was hobbling back; and then a shell
Burst slick upon the duckboards; so I fell
Into the bottomless mud, and lost the light.

The answer to 'Was it worth it?', these poets argue, has to be 'no'. But there was soon to be hope, as victory was snatched from what originally seemed like the jaws of defeat. The Germans were still as strong as ever. But the Americans were coming and the tank was finally emerging as a truly battle-changing weapon. Mud may have prevented the latter from making the difference at Passchendaele, but the next encounter, at Cambrai, would prove historic.

THE BATTLE OF AQABA AND LAWRENCE OF ARABIA

July 6th 1917

Lawrence of Arabia (Thomas Edward Lawrence) is one of the few guerrilla/resistance heroes to emerge from World War I in the battle against the Ottoman Empire in the Middle East. Other wars have had plenty of such larger-than-life characters. In World War II Churchill (a rather larger-than-life character himself) was to create a whole band of them, the Special Operations Executive, whose feats of courage behind enemy lines were to become legendary. SOE no longer exists, but the Special Air Service Regiment (the SAS) still does. However, while Churchill did all possible throughout his life to encourage mavericks and individualists to serve their country in unique and daring ways, in World War I more conventional soldiering was the norm.

The exception to this rule was T. E. Lawrence, an eccentric Oxford-trained archaeologist. His academic-based expeditions in the Middle East before 1914 suited him ideally for the work he was to do. His special task was that of gaining Arab allies once Britain and the Ottoman Empire found themselves at war a few weeks after the conflict in Europe had begun.

Lawrence spoke Arabic, and was soon linked to a group of linguists and other experts based in Cairo working out how to win the war. Until General Sir Edmund Allenby arrived in mid-1917, British activity against the Ottomans was to be a rather desultory affair. Someone as wayward or unusual as Lawrence did not find himself understood by tidier-minded officials.

The British had what they thought was a major problem. This was not so much linked to the front in Egypt. That country had been technically a British-ruled Ottoman province until 1914, when the British simply annexed it to their empire. The perceived problem was thousands of miles further to the east in the British Empire in India, often referred to simply as the Raj. Even today, India has over 130 million Muslims living there as well as Hindus and those of other faiths. From 1914 until partition at independence in 1947, the Indian Empire extended to what is now Pakistan and Bangladesh. As Churchill duly noted at the time,

Britain was the biggest Muslim power in the world.

This significant Muslim presence was to prove problematic for the British. The Ottoman Sultan also had the ancient Muslim title of Caliph (meaning successor) to the Prophet Muhammad, along with the nomenclature of Commander of the Faithful. So when he proclaimed jihad or Holy War against the British, this caused some degree of panic in those areas of the British Empire with large Muslim populations. In particular, the British were terrified of losing India, since a massive religious uprising by the tens of millions of Muslim subjects of the Raj would be impossible to suppress.

But to their great, good luck, an Arab prince with ambitions of his own now gave the British the ideal person that they needed to help deal with the Muslim problem. Emir Hussein was the hereditary governor of the two most sacred cities in Islam, Mecca and Medina. He was a bona fide Arab leader. Even better, he was known for certain to be a direct descendant of the Prophet Muhammad himself, being also a member of the same tribal group, the Hashemites. Hussein did not like Ottoman rule, and the British were desperate for a suitable Muslim to become an alternative source of religious adherence for their extensive Islamic population.

So in effect the wishes of Hussein and the British converged. Hussein declared a revolt in 1916 against the Sultan. The British, delighted to find so genealogically and religiously distinguished a Muslim on their side, decided to back him.

If one watches a film such as *Lawrence of Arabia* or reads books such as Lawrence's own memoirs, *Seven Pillars of Wisdom*, it would be easy to get the impression that most Arabs supported the revolt against their ethnically Turkish Ottoman overlords. It is certainly true that the faction in power in Constantinople – a group often nicknamed the 'Young Turks' – were far more ostensibly Turkish in how they ruled their vast empire than more recent sultans. Some sultans had deliberately emphasised non-ethnic *Islamic* unity in the place of more divisive Turkish/Arab differences.

However, recent research, albeit often controversial, has shown very clearly that the vast majority of Arabs under Ottoman rule remained entirely loyal to the Sultan. Although he was Turkish and not Arab, he was both their religious and secular overlord. There were plenty of Arabs who did join the revolt, but often for personal reasons, not because of a change of spiritual allegiance.

Not only that, but when the records and military diaries for the period were opened to public examination, it became clear that Lawrence had not always been entirely truthful or accurate in his fabled memoirs. Much was exaggerated and some of it has only a very slim degree of proximity to what his own dispatches at the time suggested had actually happened. What Lawrence had, though, and indisputably so, was flair and originality. It was this quality that so appealed to Churchill, who chose him as one of his *Great Contemporaries* in the book of that name.

Even if the Arab Revolt was not as important as first believed, it was fabulous propaganda for the British. For a natural showman such as Lawrence this gave him many opportunities, however small his actual force. When Allenby took over the military command in Egypt, he was quick to understand Lawrence's potential in a way that more conventionally minded officers had not.

So on July 6th 1917 a brave Arab force, with Lawrence in tow, successfully captured the key port of Aqaba, now a famous resort but then an important town on the Sinai Peninsula. Some of the actual details of the attack were not as dramatic as in the film, but as a propaganda victory it was glorious.

The Arabs, under the command of Hussein's son Emir Feisal, were not a major military force in terms of the defeat of the Ottoman armies in occupation of Palestine and Syria. But they could and did act as a significant irritant – for example, blowing up part of the Hejaz Railway, one of the key communication links from the Ottoman heartland to their Arab possessions.

It would be, as we shall see, the Australian and British forces under Allenby that were to conquer the Ottomans. But Lawrence and his Arab Revolt certainly played a role. And after the war Lawrence was to become famous through the film about his life by the American producer Lowell Thomas, the real creator of the legend. Lawrence remained significantly influential until 1922, when his friend Winston Churchill lost power as Colonial Secretary. He was to die in a motorbike accident, while living under a false name in 1935. But by his help in advising Churchill in 1921–1922 he was able to create a legacy that still exists in the Middle East today.

THE BATTLES OF THIRD GAZA
AND JERUSALEM

October–December 1917

Why do we have an Israel–Palestine conflict? Why is there a bloodbath in Syria? And why are these very twenty-first century questions in a book about battles fought in the First World War?

The answer is that the mess we have in the Middle East today all goes back to who conquered which piece of land back in 1917. This is not the place to discuss the intricacies of the various conflicts that have raged since the creation of Israel in 1948, and in particular since the Six-Day War in 1967, when Israelis beat the combined armies of Egypt, Syria and Jordan.

What one can say, however, is that today's Middle Eastern configuration was *not* created by two diplomats in

1916 – M. Georges Picot of France and Sir Mark Sykes of Britain – in what has become known as the 'Sykes–Picot Agreement'. That deal would have made Jerusalem an international city and would have given the oil-rich province of Mosul not to the newly British-created country of Iraq but instead to the French colony of Syria. In other words the Sykes–Picot Agreement, in which Britain and France carved up the Ottoman Empire with their then Russian ally, has nothing much to do with today's Middle East and was in effect a dead letter almost as soon as it was signed. The British Prime Minister David Lloyd George wanted Jerusalem for Britain and the oilfields of Mosul as well. There was only one way for that to happen and that was for British and imperial forces to put their boots on the ground.

And that is exactly what happened.

Up until 1917 not much was happening on the Middle Eastern Front. The British ruled Egypt, and thereby also the Suez Canal, their vital supply route through to the 'jewel in the crown' of their empire, India. But the commander of the British forces in Egypt, General Sir Archibald Murray, was rather lacklustre, and in various clashes between the start of the war in 1914 and mid-1917 not much had happened, including in two minor battles in the Gaza peninsula, the area that separates Egypt from Palestine.

Lloyd George wanted action. He had been, as we see

elsewhere, completely appalled by the carnage at the Somme in 1916, and by the failure of British troops at Arras in 1917 to make the effective breakthrough that the French had promised. While he had not agreed with Churchill over the idea of attacking the Ottoman Empire direct through the Dardanelles, he was very much an Easterner. An attack on the Ottomans would have fewer casualties than on the Western Front and, if successful, would cause grave harm to one of Germany's key allies.

He chose General Sir Edmund Allenby as commander, a cavalryman who had, at Arras, shown independence of thought and the ability to stand up to Sir Douglas Haig when necessary. Allenby was thus transferred from Flanders to the Middle East, a move that was to transform the war, but which at the time was, he thought, a demotion from the main field of battle.

Allenby soon became the kind of soldier feared and admired by his troops in equal measure. In France he was 'the Bull', a man with a known temper and of whom to be much afraid. But, his biographers concur, going to the Middle East seemed to have a liberating effect on him. He refused, unlike Murray, to run the campaigns from a luxury hotel. Then, rather like Montgomery in the desert in North Africa in 1942, he placed his own living quarters and command post closer to the front and in circumstances not as remotely grand as his predecessors.

He gained the trust of his troops, and, perhaps most importantly, of the numerous Australians under his command. As the senior Australian commander Sir Harry Chauvel put it:

> He is the most energetic commander I have yet come across. I like him immensely and he appeals to my Anzacs tremendously. He is just the kind of man we wanted here. He knows what he wants and sometimes explains it in no measured terms but he generally gets it done. The great thing is he gets about amongst the troops, looks in at hospitals . . . has a cheery word for the wounded and does not have a fit if he's not been saluted, all of which appeals to the Australians.

A British general who was liked by the ANZACs: what a contrast to the disaster at Gallipoli! How much better British/Australian/New Zealand relations would be if it were Allenby and Palestine that people remember today and not Hamilton and the catastrophe at the Dardanelles.

On October 31st 1917 the battle called Third Gaza began (Murray's two failures being the other two). This time, instead of a frontal assault on Gaza itself, which was heavily defended, Allenby attacked Beersheba, the large nearby town in the Negev desert, and thus was able to get to Gaza from a different angle. He used many techniques that were to become famous in World War II, especially that of deception, even using fake armies and spreading misleading information to make the Turks and their German allies expect the attack in the wrong place. He also managed to gain early air superiority by getting as many planes as possible from Britain from the infant Royal Flying Corps. Furthermore, unlike many generals before or since, he actually succeeded in integrating his ground troops with his air forces in a unified command and attack structure.

Third Gaza proved to be the breakthrough victory for which the British and Australian forces based in Egypt had been waiting for several years. One key component of both this success and that of subsequent parts of the campaign was Allenby's use of cavalry, which were British (mainly Yeomanry – volunteer territorial cavalry – regiments) and Australian. The trench warfare of the Western Front in Flanders had made cavalry virtually obsolete, but in the swift-moving mobile warfare of the Middle East they came into their own for perhaps the last time ever in thousands of years of military history. From the chariots of the pharaohs to the Australian light horsemen, the era of mounted warfare had been a long and great one. Allenby's troops now provided it with a final swansong.

One would have thought that victory after a three-year wait would be lauded by historians, but alas this has not always been the case. The verdict of military experts is that Allenby could have cut off the Turkish retreat and thus destroyed their entire army months earlier than he did in reality. It is possible that the critics are right, but with all reruns of great battles it is hard to tell. At least he had won, which is more than could be said for the brave but unsuccessful efforts in France or Flanders.

Within no time at all Allenby's troops were outside Jerusalem. This was, for the British Prime Minister David Lloyd George, *the* prize, especially as the endless campaigns on the Western Front had caused millions of deaths without any real victories. And although Lloyd George was a politician with an acute awareness of public opinion, the capture of Jerusalem was more to him than merely a victory to parade to the press and House of Commons as a breakthrough event. As Jill Hamilton shows in her book *God, Guns and Israel*, there was a strong streak of Christian Zionism in Lloyd George, who once claimed that, from his experience as a child in Sunday school, he knew the places in Palestine better than he did the names of many of the towns in Europe he had to discuss in Paris after the war. Writers today like Victoria Clark have shown that Christian Zionism – especially in the southern USA – is often as strong and vocal as its Jewish variant. Lloyd George's enthusiasm for the British capture of Jerusalem was thus not just a matter of trying to bring good news about the war to an exhausted British public.

The attack itself began mid-November 1917, and by December 8th British forces were almost in the city. The protecting Turkish forces had been encircled and were now routed, with the Mayor of Jerusalem handing over the keys to Allied forces on December 9th. Jerusalem, under Muslim rule since October 1187, was now back in Western hands after 730 years. British magazines such as *Punch* fondly drew the comparisons between Allenby's success and the failure of King Richard the Lionheart centuries before.

As Lloyd George was unable to attend, it was his Conservative deputy, Andrew Bonar Law, who announced the victory to the House of Commons. All the same, Lloyd George was to milk the good news as much as possible in the weeks, months and years that followed. However, too close a link with the Crusades would not, as the British realised, have been helpful. Allenby, too, did not want to be triumphalist, unlike the German Kaiser, Wilhelm II. The latter on visiting Jerusalem some years earlier (when it was under Ottoman rule) had bombastically entered the city on horseback as a self-proclaimed heir to Crusader glory.

So on December 11th 1917 the victorious Allenby, whose troops really had conquered Jerusalem, entered humbly and on foot. He proclaimed safety and toleration for all the three major faiths within the city, and carefully avoided the thorny issues now raised by the Balfour Declaration, the Foreign Secretary Arthur Balfour's promise, made the previous month to (the eminent Anglo-Jewish banker and figurehead) Lord Rothschild, of a home for Jewish people in Palestine.

The key thing here is that it was British and Australian troops who had captured Jerusalem, and with it the imagination and enthusiasm of the Western world. This instantly made a complete dead letter of the Sykes–Picot agreement, by which Jerusalem would have been under international control. What the British had conquered they would keep. Today, a century or so later, we still live with the results of their victory.

THE BATTLE OF CAPORETTO

October 24th–November 12th 1917

So many WWI battles took place between Italy and the Austro-Hungarian Empire on the plain of the Isonzo River that it is easy to get them confused. Thankfully the twelfth battle fought there is known by another name: the Battle of Caporetto.

For over two years there had been precious little movement between the two armies at war with each other, in large part because of the difficulty of the terrain. Frustratingly for the Italians, the great Austrian naval base of Trieste lay tantalisingly just beyond their grasp, and their army had lost over a million casualties in failing to get there. One such attack, the tenth battle of Isonzo, on May 12th 1917, illustrates the Italians' lack of success. The Italian general, Count Cardona, ordered a huge offensive, but by May 29th his army had hardly advanced at all. Losses were great: 75,000 Austrian troops, but over 157,000 Italians were killed and wounded.

So on August 18th the Italians tried again, launching the eleventh Battle of the Isonzo. There were two armies this time, one of them under the Duke of Aosta, a member of the Italian ruling family. This second assault failed, but the other army, under General Luigi Capello, was actually able to seize a limited amount of territory. But this was almost too successful, as his supply lines became overextended and his hitherto hopeful advance ground to a halt. Once again Italian casualties were higher than those of the Austrians, with around 148,000 for the former (with roughly 30,000 deaths) and 105,000 for the latter (with about 20,000 killed).

So by October things were even more desperate, on both sides. The Austrians, however, whose morale was not high despite surviving the attacks, had the idea of asking for help from their much more effective German allies. This made the critical difference, since the German forces, under General Otto von Below, decided that attack was the best means of defence. Their assault duly began on October 24th 1917, in the Caporetto region of the Isonzo valley (hence the name). Among the elite young German troops was an officer whose name was to become very familiar in later years: Erwin Rommel, the commander of the Afrika Korps in World War II.

This attack proved to be highly successful. With a combination of bombardment and the relatively new weapon of the flame-thrower, the German and Austrian troops were able to seize twelve miles alone on the first day. The only option that the Italians had was to flee, and to try to hold a line on the Tagliamento River.

The rapidity of their retreat to a safer position caused the attackers to slow down. On November 2nd, however, the Germans were able to relaunch, and this time the defensive line was on the River Piave, which was very close to Venice.

By this time the Italians had been thoroughly routed. Of their troops 10,000 were killed, 30,000 injured, an enormous 293,000 taken prisoner, and, perhaps worst of all, 400,000 Italian troops had simply deserted. It was, historian John Keegan notes, the 'most spectacular victory of the war since Gorlice-Tarnów in 1915'.

General Cardona was, not surprisingly, sacked and replaced by General Armando Diaz. More importantly, France and Britain decided that they had to come to Italy's aid. But there were, well into 1918, no troops to send, especially in the spring when Ludendorff began the great offensive on the Western Front that he was sure would win the war for the Germans before the Americans arrived in strength. The stalemate on the Italian Front would have to wait.

THE BATTLE OF CAMBRAI

November 20th–December 7th 1917

The Battle of Cambrai, fought in the Picardy district of northern France from November–December 1917, was the first of two battles of this name, the other one being part of the Allied counter-attacks in 1918.

Purists now like to deny that the earlier battle of Cambrai in 1917 was as historic as once claimed. The reason for its fame is that it has often been called the first tank battle in history. Technically speaking this is incorrect, as the Allies had already used earlier versions, and so prototype tanks were not utterly unknown on the battlefield.

But this is perhaps to be far too strict. It is certainly the battle in which tanks were used on a scale that had not been implemented before. Not only that, but the first day of the engagement saw tank crews acting in conjunction with infantry in a successful way that was unprecedented. Historian Correlli Barnett puts forth this view, and his argument is convincing.

The BEF was desperate to avoid the kind of carnage that had been seen at Passchendaele not long before. To the commander of the Canadian forces, Sir Julian Byng, tanks were the obvious answer. Thankfully for him, the British experts had been hard at work, and by November several hundred tanks of the latest model were ready for use.

Consequently the British assault that commenced on November 20th 1917 was a new combination of air, artillery and tank attack. No fewer than 1,000 guns blasted the German Hindenburg line. This in turn was followed with 378 tanks rumbling forward at an average of three miles an hour, with infantry following close behind. In addition some 300 planes were in action to provide cover for the ground offensive.

The tanks, however slow, were able to achieve a successful forward momentum that had eluded the conventional attacks at both the Somme and at Passchendaele. Effortlessly cutting through all the barbed wire to reach the trenches, they penetrated a full three to four miles behind the German front line. However, the German gunners were soon able to knock out several of the tanks. One particularly accurate sergeant destroyed five of them before the British infantry who were following up the rear finally killed him.

Soon the still primitive nature of the tanks proved that, while they could achieve great things in an initial attack, they were not yet developed or sophisticated enough to guarantee victory. As Correlli Barnett laments, November 20th 1917 can therefore best be summarised as a 'one-day miracle'. The German counter-attack, with no fewer than twenty-seven divisions deployed, was able to recapture all the losses made to the British on the first day. Worse still, the German offensive was able to seize ground that had hitherto been solely in the hands of the BEF.

Cambrai may have been historic, but it was not an Allied victory. However, any German celebrations were to prove premature in the long term. Their own great offensive was about to start, but it would prove to have an outcome rather different from anything that they had expected.

ON THE RUSSIAN FRONT

Lenin, the Bolsheviks, Brest-Litovsk,
Dunsterforce and Baku: 1917–1918

Be careful what you wish for, goes the old saying.

The Germans wished for a Russia that was out of the war. This they achieved on October 26th 1917 when Lenin, the new ruler of what had been tsarist Russia, issued a Peace Decree, calling on everyone to stop fighting.

How had it come to this?

Lenin and his Bolshevik faction of the Communists were opposed to the war. Strictly speaking they were the Russian Social Democrat Federation, but Marxists in any sense in which we now understand the term. Later on, Lenin was to proclaim 'socialism in one country' after attempts to export the Revolution had failed. But while in 1917 he still wanted global revolution, his principal aim was to seize power and to consolidate it. His main enemy was not the Germans but other Russians, in particular those who had supported the Russian Provisional Government that had overthrown the Tsar earlier in the year.

One could also say that the Bolsheviks' other enemy was democracy. When the Russians finally got to vote, they did not choose the Bolsheviks, but other parties, principally the Social Revolutionaries. While Lenin had seized power in the name of the people, his Marxist ideology did not permit the electorate the wrong choice. So he simply abolished the parliament and got on with his ruthless determination to keep full and sole control of the government. The tyranny of the Tsar was overthrown and substituted with that of the Communist Party, which was to rule without opposition until 1991.

Lenin had begun the year in exile in Switzerland, and he was to spend some of 1917 in Finland, notionally still part of the Russian Empire but in practice breaking away to gain independence. The Germans had no sympathies at all with his kind of ideology. Many argue that the German ruling class in fact had wanted war in 1914 in order finally to suppress or discredit socialism, and many of Lenin's views were to die in Germany in the internal conflicts that followed defeat in 1918.

Thus the German High Command, when instating Lenin as ruler of Russia, was entirely short term in its thinking. Lenin wanted to leave the war, and if he were to be in Russia, as opposed to languishing impotently in exile, he might achieve his purpose and remove one of the West's key allies. Then, with German victory in the East assured, key divisions could be transferred easily from the Eastern Front to France and Flanders, and beat the Allies. So in April 1916 he was put onto a 'sealed train' that took him from Switzerland through Germany and on to Finland Station in Petrograd, where he was met by enraptured crowds.

According to controversial and disputed statistics, some twenty million people were to die as victims of political persecution or starvation during the Soviet regime of 1917–1991. The vast bulk of these had occurred by the time of Stalin's death in 1953. In addition, tens of millions more in Central and Eastern Europe were to be ruled by Soviet puppet regimes in the Cold War of roughly 1946–1989. All these statistics exclude the People's Republic of China, which was not involved in WWI in any significant way.

In other words, a short-term German military decision, taken by people whose politics were what we would now describe as reactionary right wing as one can imagine, ended up by imposing decades of totalitarian Communism around the globe. It is perhaps, one can argue, one of the two longest-term legacies of the First World War. The second legacy is the continuing conflict in the Middle East that arose from the destruction of the Ottoman Empire.

All this, of course, was incomprehensible to the Germans of 1917. It is possibly the most dramatic example of the law of unforeseen circumstances.

In the short term the West felt that they had to do something. Large swathes of former Russian territory were now firmly under German control. Lenin was concentrating far more on fighting a civil war against his opponents than in thinking of war with the Germans. Although he did not want to surrender too much Russian territory, his military vulnerability to the anti-Bolshevik forces, sometimes nicknamed the 'White Russians' (as opposed to the Communist Red Army), meant that he did not have a strong hand to play.

So at the former border town of Brest-Litovsk negotiations began between the Germans and the Bolshevik government. But as historian John Keegan has commented, the new regime 'would not sign; neither would it fight'. For Russia the civil war was now the main conflict, with angels on neither side and with no one fighting for the kind of democracy that had flowered so very briefly in February 1917. Both sides committed the most hideous atrocities, with anything up to ten million people, many of them wholly innocent civilians, dying between 1917 and the end of the fighting in 1921. This is perhaps five or more times the number of soldiers killed during 1914–1917. We in the West can scarcely imagine carnage on such a scale. It is countless times more dreadful than even the slaughter of the Somme or Verdun.

But in the end the Germans grew tired of waiting for their Bolshevik interlocutors to sign the Brest-Litovsk agreement. On February 9th 1918 they recognised Ukrainian independence, thereby creating an enormous German puppet state free of Soviet control.

Trotsky, the former agitator turned military genius in charge of the Red Army, did his best to stall. The Bolsheviks wanted both to beat their internal enemies and at the same time not cede too much territory to the Germans. This wish to have their cake and eat it proved impossible. The Germans launched a massive campaign that, by the summer of 1918, resulted in them controlling even more of Russian soil than the Wehrmacht (a technical term for describing the German army) achieved in 1941–1943 at their peak, and with infinitely fewer casualties. Some of the most agriculturally and industrially prosperous parts of Russia were now under German rule, and their territory contained ports from Riga on the Baltic to Sevastopol in the Crimea.

By this time the Bolsheviks had realised that the game was up, finally signing a treaty with Germany at Brest-Litovsk on March 3rd 1918. Russia lost all the Baltic States (the present day Estonia, Latvia and Lithuania), all its former Polish territory (which both the Germans and Austro-Hungarians coveted), Finland and also the Ukraine. These countries have been independent since 1991 (Finland since 1918) but they had been part of Russia for centuries. The loss of so vast a region was a terrible blow.

The Allies were uncertain as to what to do. The Americans, now part of the war, did not want to fight in the vicious Russian civil war. But other countries wanted to deny as much Russian territory as they could to the Germans, and, if possible, help the White Russians regain power from the Bolsheviks. In the short term, this was to get that country back into the war, but when peace came in November 1918, for many such as Churchill it became an ideological struggle, with Bolshevik Russia the enemy of freedom. As a result, the Allies invaded parts of Russia.

British troops remained in northern Russia for some time, around the town of Archangel, from June 1918 to as late as March 1920. In the south a British/Canadian/ANZAC group known as Dunsterforce (after its commander General Lionel Dunsterville) aimed to protect the vital town of Baku. It was then one of the leading oil towns in the world, in what is now Azerbaijan. Here Dunsterforce were in conflict with everyone, including the Turks, and succeeded in preventing the Germans from seizing the town. By the end of 1918 their mission was effectively finished. In Siberia the Japanese, then an ally with Britain and France and the USA, temporarily seized parts of the country, and a group of exiled Czechs was to make a major but brief impact on the course of the civil war itself.

In the end the Bolsheviks won over their internal enemies. War weariness and increasing economic pressure meant that Western troops did not stay long on Russian soil. Trotsky was able to get the Ukraine back for Russia after the German defeat in the West and eventually large swathes of other territories that had been lost at Brest-Litovsk as well.

For the Germans it was to be a false lesson. They felt that they had won in the East. In reality they had only done so because of the implosion of old Russia caused by the Bolshevik Revolution and subsequent civil war. Nor had they, for example, tried to capture or penetrate as far as Moscow, as they aimed to do in very different circumstances in 1941. In 1918 they had the Ukrainian nationalists and the Cossack population of that region very much on their side. In the Baltic region, for example, they were even pro-Semitic, granting honorary German status to many of the large Jewish minority there. Come 1941 all these lessons would be forgotten, with over 27 million deaths between 1941 and 1945 to prove it.

PART FIVE

THE ROAD TO FINAL VICTORY

MAGNIFICENT MEN IN THEIR FLYING MACHINES

The Air War

The First World War was the first major conflict fought in the sky as well as at sea and on land. Flight itself was an early twentieth-century invention, and so the fighter aces were pioneers in every sense of the word. No one could ever have fought like them before; they had no role models upon whom to base their own actions.

But in one sense the notion of brave fighters taking each other on thousands of feet above the trenches below brought back memories of a more heroic age. With hundreds of thousands of infantry killing and being killed in a struggle of attrition between the trenches, war had become industrial in scale, devoid of the personal. Fighter exchanges, however, brought back memories of knights jousting, of brave individual combat, of one lone swordsman pitted in a duel to the death against another. The 57,000 casualties on the first day of the Somme were too much to take in. But one ace against another was like Roman gladiators at the Circus Maximus – battle on a human scale. And it is no coincidence that the British pilots of the Royal Flying Corps nicknamed the group centred around their main adversary as 'Richthofen's Flying Circus'.

Manfred von Richthofen of Germany was the flying ace par excellence. (An ace was someone who had scored a minimum of five kills in aerial combat; he went on to score a remarkable eighty.) He was called the 'Red Baron' after the fact that in 1917 he painted his planes (then called flying machines) bright scarlet. He continued to create havoc in the ranks of his opponents until he was shot down himself on April 21st 1918 by the Royal Flying Corps ace from Canada, Roy Brown – and possibly also by Australian troops shooting up from the ground. His successor as chief of the 'Flying Circus' was to become notorious for other reasons: his name was Hermann Goering, whose bravery and fighting prowess in the First World War gave huge credence later on to his post-war political associates, the Nazi Party.

Soon many Allied aces became heroes as well. The two French fighters Charles Nungesser and René Fonck were figures of glamour as well as aerial prowess. Fonck was the most successful, managing to achieve seventy-five kills, and in his case died many years later and peacefully in 1953. He was nicknamed the 'Ace of Aces'.

The Royal Flying Corps was the main British wing, and the first to be granted full recognition as an independent branch of the Armed Forces when it merged with the smaller Royal Navy Air Service straight after the war, becoming the Royal Air Force. Writers have noted that the British ethos was somewhat different from that of the French and Germans, with bragging about the number of aces gained as being somehow bad form. Despite this, the infant Royal Flying Corps did produce not a few aces of its own, and of a very British kind.

We normally associate such prowess with the products of the independent school system, brave chaps doing their bit, and of these Albert Ball was perhaps the exemplar. Ball won the highest medal for bravery, the Victoria Cross, and was tragically killed in action in 1917 having achieved forty-four kills. But Britain's top ace was Edward Mannock, with seventy-three kills, a strong socialist of a distinctly unprivileged background, who was to die in July 1918 not in a dogfight in the air but shot down by ground fire. James McCudden was from a working-class background and rose up from the ranks, losing his life in July 1918 in an ordinary air accident, a sad end for a man who had scored fifty-seven kills in his short but meteoric career. The other major ace was William Bishop, a Canadian with seventy-two kills, who happily survived the war and was instrumental in the establishment of the Royal Canadian Air Force.

The USA came late to the war, so just achieved one notable ace, Eddie Rickenbacker, famous back home as an Indianapolis 500 racing driver. Transferring his skills to the air, he joined the 'Hat in the Ring' fighter squadron and was able to achieve a very respectable twenty-six kills before the war finished.

With its connotations of medieval chivalry the fighter pilots were able to have a clean and perhaps even wholesome image. But as the millions of civilians who were massacred from the air in the bombing campaigns of World War II can attest, air warfare has a dark side to it as well. In fact, the Second World War was to be the first conflict in history where the *civilian* death toll far exceeded that of the military.

Thankfully the First World War was still in a more innocent age. There were some bombing raids, however, even if not remotely on the scale of what was to come later. At the start of the conflict these came in the form of attacks by Zeppelins, the vast German-designed airships that at the time seemed at the very cutting edge of aviation technology. (It was not until a series of terrible accidents in the 1930s that people realised how dangerous such airships could be.)

Zeppelins, though, were not really designed to be bombers. The devastation caused by one raid on London in September 1915, while causing much shock at the time, was nowhere near the scale of the Blitz twenty-five years later. Nonetheless, for an island nation such as Britain, air raids meant the end of the immunity the country had hitherto been able to achieve, and were therefore a major shock. Soon the United Kingdom worked on bombing capabilities of its own, and in the form of planes rather than airships. The de Havilland works near London were soon able to produce a flying machine with the ability to drop four bombs per mission. And it was these machines, rather than the airships, that were to be a forecast of wars to come.

Historian John Keegan has suggested that while exciting and new, the air forces of World War I probably did not make a key difference to winning the conflict. They were of much help to the armies with whom they worked, however, since aerial reconnaissance enabled military commanders on the ground to know more about enemy dispositions than had ever been the case before. In that alone they could have made a critical difference, especially when in late 1918 the armies in Flanders ceased to be trench-bound and a war of movement was able to begin at last.

THE LUDENDORFF OFFENSIVE
OR KAISER BATTLE

March 21st–July 18th 1918

By the beginning of 1918 it was obvious to the German High Command based in Belgium that they had to get a major offensive under way against the British and French before US troops began to land in Europe in serious numbers. The prospect of over a million American forces to add to Allied numbers concentrated German minds considerably. In addition, the Russian Front had now turned to the advantage of the Central Powers with the Bolshevik government having taken Russia out of the war. Germany was thus able to bring many divisions from the Eastern Front to Western Europe, in the hope of delivering the longed-for knockout blow.

The main enemy would be the British, and it was upon

them that the main thrust of the Kaiserschlacht (Kaiser Battle) would be delivered. (While that was the formal name it is most often known as the Spring or Ludendorff Offensive.) If the United Kingdom were out of the conflict, and if the Americans had not yet landed in strength, then France would be finished and Germany could still win the war.

Many uncertainties can be noted in that wish list. Furthermore, as commentators and historians have pointed out, the attempts in 1916 and 1917 by Allied attacking forces to batter themselves against German defences had proved futile, at the cost of catastrophic numbers of casualties. What reason was there that a German offensive against British defences, coupled with diversionary action against the French, would prove any different or less costly?

The first of four planned attacks, 'Michael', began with the usual massive bombardment of over one million shells on March 21st 1918. Three German armies attacked the British in the area around the Somme on a sixty-mile front. Rawlinson's army was duly battered and, as the German commander Ludendorff had hoped, the French were nervous about losing British allies. Pétain, to the BEF's fury, expressed himself more anxious about the defences of Paris than he was about how to shore up his ally's armies.

Within two weeks the Germans had managed to create a large forty-mile salient into Allied-held territory. But as one American historian has written, this attack was a 'tactical success . . . but a strategic failure'. As with so many such offensives during that war, the German troops had driven well ahead of their supply lines, and so further and faster than it would have been prudent to attempt.

Then the British and French leaders convened near Amiens, at a place called Doullens. Haig had to admit that one of his armies had disintegrated, and Pétain expressed his fears again for Paris. But Marshal Foch, the French senior commander, stood firm as a rock. 'We must not now retire a single inch,' he proclaimed. On April 3rd he was given overall command of both British and French soldiers, and his resolution was to save the day.

The Germans had not just overstretched themselves. They now made a key strategic error. Instead of one great hammer blow against the British, they effectively split their offensive into three prongs, none of which, historians have noted 'would be strong enough to achieve a breakthrough'. Then, on April 4th the Australians launched a massive counter-attack and the original German juggernaut that had been launched in March was finally halted. It had come at a cost, with 255,000 Allied casualties (now including Americans for the first time) and roughly 239,000 for the German invaders.

Ludendorff, however, refused to give up, and on April 11th he launched a second massive assault against the British. But this time Sir Douglas Haig was firm and resolute, issuing one of the most famous battle instructions of the war. 'With our backs to the wall, and believing in the justice of our cause, each one of us must fight on to the end . . . Every position must be held to the last man. There must be no retirement.' Since Foch did not have any spare French troops to send to the BEF, the British and Empire troops were on their own.

One of the rare tank battles of the war took place on April 24th, just south of the former Ypres battlefield. British tanks proved superior to those of the Germans and the latter's attack was successfully pushed back. So by April 29th Ludendorff was compelled to cancel this attack as well. This was in part due to the great bravery of American troops, who fought alongside the British in what has been named the Battle of Lys, a subset of the overall offensive. The American Expeditionary Force had begun to make a difference.

Having failed utterly against the British, Ludendorff was determined that something should be done, and on May 27th he launched 'Blücher', named for the great Prussian general who had helped the British beat Napoleon at the Battle of Waterloo in 1815. Over two million shells were used to batter the French positions.

This proved an initial success, since the Germans were able to progress a good twenty miles just on the first day. Within three days they had reached the River Marne, site of the great Allied turnaround victory in 1914 and only fifty-six miles from Paris.

Here all the Allies came to the aid of the French, including now two US divisions. The Marine Corps sprang into action, winning a major victory over the Germans at the Battle of Belleau Wood on June 4th. This was to prove the costliest US Marine battle in history until the much bigger conflicts in which they were to be engaged in the Pacific after 1941. Rather touchingly, the French were so grateful that they renamed the area Bois de la Brigade de Marine.

The day before, Ludendorff had already decided that even this attack was now futile. He had lost over 100,000 casualties in that offensive alone. Although many forces had been transferred from the former Eastern Front to fight in France, the German casualty rate was now getting far higher than their natural replacement rate for new recruits.

The Germans still did not give up fully, however. On June 9th Ludendorff announced another offensive, this time based on the River Matz, to increase the size of the German salient. But this too was broken off, and rather rapidly, by French and American forces, as early as June 14th.

Everything seemed to be failing for the Germans. Ludendorff dithered for a whole month, unsure whether to try to capture Paris, or to push the British out of Flanders. On July 15th he finally made up his mind. He committed all his remaining forces to an attack against the French, in what has been called the Second Battle of the Marne.

This time not only were the French ready for them, but five US Divisions as well: 28,000 Americans all keen and eager to fight. On July 18th the Allies launched a massive counter-offensive that had the desired effect. The Germans were once again halted.

German losses were becoming unacceptably high. Their army was now down from 5.1 million to 4.2 million in just six months, and their country simply did not have the replacements necessary were Ludendorff to continue his offensive programme. Siren voices within the German military command were now pressing for their forces to be withdrawn to defensive lines last held in 1917. Furthermore, as historian John Keegan notes, the Germans were hopeless when it came to making proper and effective use of tank technology – what he describes as 'one of their worst military miscalculations of the war'. The French and British by contrast were developing new ranges of tanks all the time, with production levels to match the demand. The Germans were still using horses.

Then on August 30th 1918 the American Expeditionary Force was constituted as an independent military command, under its experienced leader General John Pershing. Back on March 21st the situation for the Allies had looked hopeless. Now the entire picture had changed, and the Western Allies were poised for victory.

ARMAGEDDON TO DAMASCUS

Allenby's Autumn 1918 Campaign

General Allenby, having captured Jerusalem, now had to wait to follow up on his great victory of the year before. There were some minor raids into what is now Jordan and Lebanon, but not on the scale of 1917. The Ludendorff offensive in Europe meant that some of the best troops in Palestine now had to go to Flanders to fight the Germans. Since to the 'Westerners', those in Britain whose concentration was solely on beating the main German enemy in Europe, the very presence of so many British and Australian troops in the Middle East was foolishness, it is perhaps surprising that Allenby's campaign was allowed to continue at all. But so great had the propaganda and moral victory been of capturing Jerusalem that he was, after all, permitted to stay.

So it was with a smaller force, some of which came from the West Indies and Africa, that Allenby was able to begin the final phase of his campaign in the autumn of 1918. He was also to make very effective use of the infant Royal Flying Corps, whose planes were to terrify the Turkish troops.

The first major battle is often named after Megiddo, the great Jewish battle site (in 609 BC) subsequently made famous by the prophecy of Armageddon, the Last Battle, in the Book of Revelation. It was in fact a series of engagements, in the vicinity of Megiddo, taking place between September 19th and 25th. Its nomenclature, while perhaps misleading, bestows upon it a resonant name which seemed to give the battle extra cachet. Many sources (including Wikipedia, and the multi-volume history of the British cavalry by Lord Anglesey) give detailed descriptions of the various conflicts that come under the Megiddo umbrella. When Allenby was given a peerage and created a Field Marshal in 1919 it is significant that he chose as his title Viscount Allenby of Felixstowe *and Megiddo* rather than commemorating any of his other victories.

Once again the artillery bombardment shattered Turkish resistance and the various cavalry regiments that had remained in the Middle East wiped out what remained. It was one of the most successful Allied victories of the war, with remarkably few casualties in comparison with the carnage in Flanders.

Finally came the capture of Damascus – by Australian mounted troops – with the assault beginning around October 1st. One of the greatest myths of the war, propagated heavily by T. E. Lawrence himself, and thus in the much later film *Lawrence of Arabia*, is that Arab forces under commander Emir Feisal were responsible for this victory. Ironically the British fostered this myth even at the time, to their own later discredit. When Feisal was forced by the French to quit Damascus in 1920, the legend was that it was Feisal's legions that had liberated the city (the propaganda). The truth, that it had been the valiant Australian cavalry, was held against the United Kingdom, as they were seen to have betrayed their brave Arab allies to the perfidious French.

Academic research has now proved what was long suspected by the Middle East specialist, the late Elie Kedourie, over fifty years ago. We now know that the 'capture' of Damascus was stage-managed from the beginning to give the outward appearance of an Arab victory. In fact the truth was that it could never have happened but for the forces under Allenby's command. So confused did the situation become at one point that the Australians went into Damascus and captured it anyway, regardless of the plan to make it look as if the city had fallen to Feisal's forces.

This issue is important for us in the twenty-first century, and not as arcane as it might seem. At the time

of writing this chapter, there is much conflict in Syria
in what seems to be an intractable war, with well over
100,000 Syrians from different backgrounds killed and
millions displaced or exiled altogether from their homes.
Therefore the question regarding Syria, of who captured
it and how in 1918, is not an argument of interest only to
historians. Rather it is of profound relevance to millions
of people who live – and increasingly who are being killed
– in that exact same region today. The effects of what
was accomplished by courageous Australian cavalry under
Allenby's command thus resonates a century later in our
own time.

People who attempt to explain what happened in
Syria back in 1918 argue that the British needed Feisal
for political purposes and that Feisal needed the British
and British Empire troops for military reasons. Feisal
could not defeat the Turks alone – remember, most Arabs
supported their fellow Muslim Ottoman overlords and
not the Hashemites. In turn the British needed Feisal
as cover for taking Syria away from the French. If the
British had been capturing Damascus for themselves,
they would have had no reason but to hand it over to
France, who wanted it. But if it looked as if a popular
uprising of Arabs had captured Damascus, then the
British could pretend that they were simply supporting
local people and had no choice but to recognise the
situation on the ground.

Thus as academics now argue, a deception was prepared, one to which Allenby was, it seems, not privy in advance but with which he went along as a simple soldier who followed orders. (So far as one can see, no biographer has suggested otherwise.) But the truth was that his leadership and successful command had made the whole enterprise possible – if in late 1918 the British had still been stuck behind the Suez Canal in Egypt, all the plotting in the world would have made no difference.

A few weeks later on October 30th the Ottomans signed an armistice at Mudros, which ended the war. Allenby had succeeded, at minimal cost, in achieving victory.

THE BATTLE OF VITTORIO VENETO

October 24th–27th 1918

If the Austrians could get German troops to help them against the Italians in 1917, the British and French could eventually bestow the same favour on their hitherto lacklustre Italian allies. The Austrians had tried, in June 1918, at the Battle of the Piave, to repeat their success of 1917 at Caporetto, but nature was against them, as floods halted their offensive.

By October 1918 General Armando Diaz, the Italian commander, had forces from Britain and France as well as Italian troops. He was able to launch his campaign, just as the Germans were cracking on the Western Front in Flanders and as the Austro-Hungarian Empire was disintegrating. In the latter case, the different ethnic groups increasingly preferred independence to being part of a multinational empire. On October 2nd the young Austrian Emperor Karl had attempted to find a way out of the war by approaching the Americans, but by this time his subjects were in an advanced state of revolt. The fragile empire, ruled by the Habsburgs for centuries, was now in its death throes.

All was not entirely over, however. The Austrians were not intending to go down without giving the Italians a hard time. On October 23rd, at the Battle of Monte Grappa, still loyal Austrian soldiers were able to inflict some 17,000 casualties on the Italians before themselves being compelled to retreat.

Diaz and his allies were determined, though, to keep to the attack. So on October 24th the British, French and Italians began the offensive at Vittorio Veneto. And just in time an American regiment was able to join, making the war on this front a fully Allied effort.

Finally success came, just as the war in Europe was coming to an end. The Allies were able to cross back over the River Piave and by October 30th they were breaching the Austrian lines. By November 1st the Italians had some major gains and on November 3rd British and French forces seized the historic town of Trent. And finally, after three years of failure, Italian troops, along with their allies, captured Trieste.

On that day the Austrians decided to surrender. The

great multi-ethnic Habsburg Empire disintegrated into its several component parts, with new countries being created that had never existed before. While Trieste itself became Italian, much of the hinterland was awarded to a state that was wholly new – the Kingdom of the Serbs, Croats and Slovenes, soon renamed Yugoslavia. Today that nation has also ceased to exist, along with Austria-Hungary, and the region of Vittorio Veneto is now divided between Italy and the brand-new country of Slovenia.

Italian success in 1918 meant that they could enter the peace process as victors – though their total lack of martial success up until 1918 suggests that they were fortunate to do so. It was a lesson that the rather brutal Fascist regime that soon took power there was to overlook.

THE HUNDRED DAYS

The Allies, the USA and the Road to Victory

Numbers matter. It may seem as if the Allies were doomed in 1918, with the German offensive getting close to Paris, and with Germany now in effect having to fight only on one front, in Flanders and France. But look at the statistics of American troop arrivals in Europe for 1918:

March: 64,000

April: 121,000

May: 214,000

June: 238,000

July: 247,000

August: 280,000

September: 263,000

October: 227,000

Total: 1,654,000

Of these troops, some 193,611 were wounded and 50,476 were killed – most of the latter, as we shall see, in a single engagement at Meuse-Argonne. Tragically more Americans were to die of the influenza epidemic (roughly over 57,000) than died in combat.

People disagree on how well the Americans fought, and on how good General Pershing was once he was able to exercise effective command of his own forces. Everyone, though, remembers how brave most US soldiers were as individuals. When US Marine Lloyd Williams, the first Virginian to be killed in the war, was asked to retreat just before his death, he scorned the command with the now immortal words: 'Hell, we only just got here!'

Williams might have been foolhardy – he died eleven days after making this remark. But the sheer size of the American force, whatever skills the rookie soldiers possessed, scared the daylights out of the Germans, and reduced the morale even of their leadership. As historian Correlli Barnett has said, these figures 'spelt defeat for Germany'.

By this time most British, French and Germans had lost their entire original force to casualties in many of their fighting units – the professional soldiers of 1914 had all been killed or injured and even the conscripts had been replaced many times over in a single regiment. But the American troops, however inexperienced, were all new and fresh. The Germans simply could not have the replacement rate to combat the new arrivals. Germany did not have remotely the population necessary of those born at the right time to serve in the army. American manpower was vast and even by victory had not been anywhere near fully tapped. Tens of thousands more could have been added from this American source.

Disputes on exactly how well the American Expeditionary Force, the AEF, fought once engaged with the enemy are thus irrelevant, not to forget condescending. Contrast how well the much bigger US army fought against the Japanese and Germans by 1944–1945, compared with their shaky start in North Africa in 1942–1943. Given time and more combat experience the AEF would have been no different. But the size of the American force alone made a vast difference, even if much of the successful fighting of the last hundred days was carried out by, for example, equally heroic but also battle-hardened Australian, New

Zealand and Canadian troops. Many argue that their fighting prowess carried the forces under Haig's command all the way to victory by November 1918. Indeed some have described the last phase of the war with the nickname 'Canada's Hundred Days', although the Australian forces were equally heroic.

Historians have outlined three crucial advantages that the Allies had by 1918 that made all the difference between slaughter and wasted lives in 1916–1917 and victory a year later. These were as David Stevenson reminds us 'flexible logistics, command of the seas and a powerful industrial base'.

Logistics is often neglected in wartime stories, but it cannot be forgotten here if we are to understand how the Allies won. (Strictly speaking the USA was an Associate Power, not a formal Ally, but it is simpler if technically inaccurate to combine them altogether as 'Allies'.) If one considers simply transport, for example, David Stevenson also points out that 'almost as many supply trains reached the front as during the five months of the Somme'.

We tend to look at military commanders when we consider who wins battles. But civilians can make all the difference. Most of us have never heard of a businessman called Sir Eric Geddes. But his appointment as Director of Transport for the BEF in 1916–1917 proved revolutionary, in that he was able to get the new troops to the right place at the right time. A general might have a wonderful plan, but if there are traffic delays and endless chaos preventing soldiers from getting to where they should be, then the best laid plans can be for nought.

Without command of the seas, the American troops would never have reached Europe to make so critical a difference in finishing the war. Naval power also ensured that armaments were able to reach their destination. This is not to say that German U-boats were ineffective, but that by 1918 the Allies were doing well and that Room 40 at the Admiralty was able to break U-boat codes in a way that reflected the later success of Bletchley Park in World War II.

Finally, the Allied industrial base was unsurpassed, especially that of France and the United Kingdom. The USA also helped but their War Industries Board, founded in 1917, did not really get going until the spring of 1918. It was French and British improvement in the quality and quantity of shells that made the difference on the battlefield. The USA was instrumental in feeding the hungry Allied populations and in greatly strengthening the blockade of Germany, causing considerable starvation in that country. The Allies maintained this blockade well into 1919 until the new German Republic agreed to sign the Treaty of Versailles.

None of these factors are directly connected to the fighting on the Western Front, but all made a tremendous impact, and gave the British, French and Americans the distinct edge over the Central Powers.

These substantial changes in support strategy explain how the Allies won in 1918 with many of the same leaders they had in the days of carnage in 1916–1917. It was not that the commanders themselves had improved, but that the logistics that enabled them to use what they possessed had done so immeasurably, along with what we should consider the biggest difference of all: the arrival in huge numbers of forces from the USA. And in military terms, the decision to give Marshal Foch command over the armies from all the Allied countries meant that Allied efforts were fully co-ordinated in a way in which they had not been before. The theory of unity via the Supreme War Council was now replaced by the practice of a leader who actually knew what he was doing.

In the dramatic words of Correlli Barnett: 'At 4.35 a.m. on the 18th July the pendulum of war began finally to swing against Germany.' The Allies now had their act together. Foch's attack on the German salient, created by the latter's spring victories, was now filled by successful French and American forces, supported by 400 French tanks as part of the assault. Within two days over six miles of German territory had been taken. As Hindenburg confessed in his memoirs, from 'the purely military point of view it was of the greatest and most fateful importance that we had lost the initiative to the enemy'.

Then on August 8th Haig and Rawlinson launched a British and Empire offensive on the Somme that restored their reputations and began the continuous forward surge that would lead the BEF all the way to final victory in November. There were Americans under Haig and also key Australian and Canadian forces that alongside the US divisions were all to prove the bravest of the brave. Crucially this time there were 342 heavy tanks and 72 of a lighter, new design. These powerful new weapons, well integrated with the infantry, now launched the attack at 4.20 a.m.

This was no Battle of the Somme. The Allied forces were able successfully to advance many in a single day, and with just 6,000 or so Australian and Canadian casualties. Germans now surrendered in droves, and as Ludendorff lamented, 'August 8th was the black day of the German army in the history of this war'. Within two days of the BEF victories, Ludendorff had begun to wonder if the Germans could hold out at all. By the end of the month the Allies were at the edge of the Hindenburg Line itself and the German border.

CONCLUSION

The Shadow of the Somme

The war was over. Figures are as always much disputed, but it is possible that the Allies lost over five million and the Central Powers something over four million soldiers to death. Many of the wounded survivors, because of the state of medical treatment at the time, had injuries from which no real recovery was possible. The mental trauma of war was not then understood as it was by the standards of a later time.

Whichever way one looks at the casualty totals, they were vast in comparison to anything that had happened in living memory. The Napoleonic Wars, which had ended 130 years earlier, had lasted far longer, but by 1918 they had long since been forgotten. The deeper trauma of the

Thirty Years' War in Central Europe was now centuries past. No one alive in 1918 could therefore recall anything with quite such an impact. Indeed, one could argue that there had never been such widespread trauma, since even the Mongol invasions of medieval times had not penetrated that far into Central and Western Europe.

Whole forests have been felled to write libraries of books on how the ending of World War I led to the origins of World War II. Decades on, historians still do not agree on how this happened, though most would concur that there is a direct correlation between the two events. But most of that discussion, albeit fascinating, does not relate directly to the *battles* of World War I, the theme of our book. The national trauma that the cumulative effect of the war created lived on for generations afterwards. Allan Mallinson has described what he calls the 'Shadow of the Somme'. It was not really until after the war itself was over, he argues, let alone at the time in 1916, that the full impact of those 57,000 casualties on the first day of the battle truly sank in to military and national consciousness. Only then did the full horror of the carnage become truly apparent. The same of course can be said of the French equivalent at Verdun, where the casualties had been greater and the shock commensurately worse.

We now find it very easy to blame the appeasers of the interwar period for the outbreak of World War II – mediocre politicians such as Neville Chamberlain, who saw everything through the narrow perspective of his days as a provincial mayor. Churchill was right, we say, and Hitler should have been resisted from the outset.

Morally speaking Churchill was entirely right. Hitler was no simple German nationalist but a Nazi monster of wholly evil proportions only rarely seen in history. The slaughter of six million wholly innocent Jews makes the casualties even of the Somme seem minor, as do the twenty-seven million Soviet citizens, military and civilian, wiped out on the Eastern Front between 1941 and 1945.

But in one sense this is the problem – we see World War I completely through the prism of the far worse Second World War and its fifty-five to perhaps eighty million deaths, and the forty-four-year Cold War that followed from it.

The saying 'hindsight is a wonderful thing' has been attributed to David Beckham. Whoever originally did utter those words is profoundly correct. What we forget altogether about the period 1918–1939 is that the leaders and statesmen of that era had no idea – except perhaps for Winston Churchill – of what was about to happen. For them the key thing to avoid was what *had happened*, and that was the carnage and horror of the Western Front. The fact that an infinitely worse conflagration was to follow, ending in the unthinkable terror of the atomic bomb, would have been entirely alien and quite fantastic to them, in the original sense of that term.

So it is hardly surprising then that democratically elected

Western politicians did all possible for that twenty-year interim period to avoid a future war. Pacifism in the light of Adolph Hitler now seems utterly immoral, but at the time it seemed to be the only responsible course of action for a democracy to take. Who would want a repetition of July 1st 1916? Or of the carnage of Verdun? As Churchill discovered to his cost, to argue for rearmament and for a posture of war-readiness against Nazi Germany, while entirely sensible now, was at the time electoral suicide.

In addition, Britain emerged from 1918 virtually broke. What is interesting is that when he was in office from 1918 to 1922 (including as Secretary of State for War 1918–1921) and again from 1924 to1929, few people were more enthusiastic for defence *cuts* and drastic reduction in British military downsizing as Winston Churchill.

After 1925 it looked as if Germany had discovered peace and prosperity. Since the Nazi vote was throughout this earlier period almost laughably minuscule, who would have said that the 'Ten-Year Rule' that proposed that Britain would not be at war for at least ten years was short-sighted or foolish? No one in 1925 would have ever predicted that an obscure Bavarian rabble-rouser called Adolph Hitler would be in power within eight years and Germany transformed into a monster without parallel for centuries.

This is not to excuse the interwar politicians and military leaders – far from it. But it does at least help us to explain and to understand them, and to show why the idea of yet another war with more deaths, casualties and battles of the Somme or Verdun was so horrific.

Over many decades the debate about the causes of the Second World War has attributed blame to the mistakes of the peacemakers at Versailles. There is general consensus that there is a link between what happened in 1919 and what started twenty years later in 1939. But this is too simplistic. For unless we understand the trauma of what happened in 1914–1918, then we fail to grasp what the statesmen were up to in Paris in 1919 in the peace treaty with Germany. The horrors of the trenches were in the minds of all the Allied politicians and diplomats as they strove to create a world in which such horrors would never recur. They failed, as we now know. But it was that shadow hanging over all of them that led to their decisions, and thus to the tragic outcome two decades later in 1939.

Allan Mallinson has made another important point about the shadow of the Somme, one that, he argues, extends right down into the British army of the twenty-first century. This too is a legacy of the traumas of the Western Front and of the battles of the First World War.

During the Second World War, British commanders were often told by infuriated and more gung-ho American leaders that they were far too risk-averse in launching attacks against the enemy. There is the iconic story of irate Americans during the attempt to capture the Bridge at

Arnhem discovering British tank crews having a break for a cup of tea!

Much has been made by historians such as Max Hastings of this lack of martial vigour by British troops, in comparison to their more aggressive German counterparts. To be fair to his compatriots, Hastings does point out that the British are by nature a democratic and tolerant people, unlike the Germans whose loyalty to the Nazi leadership in World War II drove them on despite the crumbling of their world in the face of Allied victory.

This is all possibly true, and there is a good case that can be made. But writers such as Mallinson are also right to say that the tolerance for high casualties that marked out World War I was conspicuous by its absence in the Second World War. It is often said that the captains and majors of the First World War were the generals of the Second. These were leaders who, so unlike the commanders of 1914–1918, whose only experience was of colonial warfare, were able to lead as they did precisely because they, as young officers, had encountered the realities of modern war in the trenches of Flanders. Britain had many good and effective generals in World War II and this is surely why.

But they were risk-averse – and in a way that, Mallinson argues, is still true of the British army in the twenty-first century. They had seen the first day of the Somme – and unlike thousands of their fallen comrades had lived to tell the tale. This has been called 'survivor's guilt', but that description is perhaps rather unfair. They were not so much guilt-ridden at having survived, but determined that, should war break out again, the kind of attrition warfare that led to so many often quite needless casualties should not happen again. They knew that most of the soldiers under their command were civilian conscripts, ordinary folk forced into uniform by the exigencies of war.

Haig and others knew this in theory, but having only served in a volunteer army, in which every soldier had actually chosen to be in uniform prior to 1914, they would not have realised its implications *in practice* and what it meant to be a scared civilian forced to fight against a fanatical enemy. Yes, Montgomery, Alexander, Slim, Horrocks in the Second World War and others wanted to beat the Germans and end the war, but because of their own experiences at the Somme and similar battles, they aimed to do so with the minimum of casualties to their own side.

Consequently, although the British fought valiantly in World War II, they did not do so with the sometimes almost reckless boldness of their American allies. On the Eastern Front, where eighty-five per cent or more of German casualties occurred, the Soviet leaders, such as Marshal Zhukov, succeeded. They did so, however, with a total disregard for human life and the suffering of their men that makes Haig look mild in comparison. No British World War I leader showed anything remotely like the utter callousness for casualties and death that was the hallmark of all the World War II Red Army commanders. Well over twenty times as many Soviet troops died in 1941–1945 than all the deaths and casualties combined of British armed forces in World War I. The Red Army shot more men for cowardice than *all* British casualties in the Second World War.

The shadow of the Somme is still with us, and has changed how we in Britain think forever. Surely this is for the good, so that no generation of soldiers will ever have to suffer the fate of those who died on July 1st 1916. We won that war, so they did not die needlessly. And their surviving comrades ensured that their successors would not have to die in such terrible circumstances ever again. D-Day, despite all the fears of the British chiefs of staff in 1944, was no repetition of the Somme and indeed there never has been such a horror since. For that, too, those who died in July 1916 did not die in vain.

WHO'S WHO OF KEY WORLD WAR I COMMANDERS

This is a summary of selected key commanders that appear throughout the book. They are listed with the titles they had during the war. Many victorious leaders were given peerages by the British government after the war and these can be rather complex for readers unfamiliar with this system of honours.

Allenby, Field Marshal Sir Edmund, 1861–1936 (*British*) A cavalry commander in the BEF, then of the Third Army, before going to Egypt in 1917 as commander-in-chief of the victorious Egyptian Expeditionary Force.

Beatty, Admiral of the Fleet Sir David, 1871–1936 (*British*) Commander of the First Battle Cruiser squadron at Jutland and then Commander-in-Chief of the Grand Fleet.

Brusilov, General Aleksei, 1853–1926 (*Russian*) Commander of the Eighth Army in 1914, of the South-West Front in 1916 and of a major offensive in 1917.

Bulow, Field Marshal Karl von, 1846–1921 (*German*) In command of the 2nd Army in 1914. After winning in Belgium by capturing Liege and Namur, his army became stymied thirty miles from Paris. A heart attack forced his retirement in 1915.

Byng, Field Marshal Sir Julian, 1862–1935 (*British*) Byng was in Egypt when the war began but was quickly transferred to the Western Front for First Ypres. He was sent to Gallipoli to clean up the mess caused by Hamilton *q.v.* and in May 1916 he was put in charge of the Canadian Army Corps on the Western Front. In April 1917 his troops secured a major victory at Vimy Ridge. In

June 1917 he was given command of the Third Army and as such was involved in the successful Hundred Days in 1918.

Cardona, Marshal Luigi, 1850–1928 (*Italian*) Began his war in May 1914 as the Italian Chief of Staff. He kept his country in the war despite the stalemate on the Isonzo Front with Austria, but the disastrous defeat at Caporetto in 1917 ended his career.

Conrad von Hötzendorf, Field Marshal Count Franz, 1852–1925 (*Austrian*) The Austro-Hungarian Chief of the General Staff.

Currie, General Sir Arthur, 1875–1933 (*Canadian*) Commander of the Canadian Corps on the Western Front.

Diaz, Marshal Armando, 1861–1928 (*Italian*) Chief of Staff after 1917.

Falkenhayn, General Erich von, 1861–1922 (*German*) Served as Chief of Staff 1914–1916 when after the failure to break through at Verdun he was transferred to Romania and then to Palestine.

Foch, Field Marshal Ferdinand, 1851–1929 (*French*) Served as a General in different places on the Western Front until becoming Chief of the General Staff in 1917 and Allied Commander-in-Chief in 1918.

French, Field Marshal, Sir John 1852–1925 (*British*) The unsuccessful Commander-in-Chief of the BEF 1914–1915.

Haig, Field Marshal Sir Douglas, 1861–1928 (*British*) Began the war as a Corps Commander, then as the head of the First Army, becoming Commander-in-Chief of the BEF in late 1915 for the rest of the war.

Hamilton, General Sir Ian, 1853–1947 (*British*) The unsuccessful commander of the Allied (including ANZAC) troops at Gallipoli March–October 1915.

Hindenburg, Field Marshal Paul von, 1847–1934 (*German*) Hindenburg came out of retirement to command the victorious German troops on the Eastern Front in 1914 and in 1916 became Chief of the General Staff in charge of all operations including those on the Western Front.

Jellicoe, Admiral of the Fleet Sir John, 1859–1935 (*British*) Commanded the Grand Fleet at Jutland in 1916 and then as First Sea Lord 1916–1917.

Joffre, Marshal Joseph, 1852–1931 (*French*) The French Chief of General Staff from 1914–1916.

Kemal Pasha, General Mustafa (Ataturk), 1881–1938 (*Turkish*) The effective Turkish leader of the Ottoman forces at Gallipoli.

Kitchener, Field Marshal the Earl (Horatio Herbert), 1850–1916 (*British*) One of Britain's leading war heroes when he became Secretary of State for War in 1914. He died when his ship was sunk at sea in 1916.

Kluck, General Alexander von, 1846–1936 (*German*) Commanded the 1st Army in 1914, including the unsuccessful manoeuvre that many claim led the Germans to fail to capture Paris. He retired in 1915.

Kornilov, General Lavr, 1870–1918 (Russian) The Provisional government's Commander-in-Chief during the latter's brief time in office between the first and second Russian Revolutions.

Lawrence, T. E., 1888–1935 (*British*) A maverick archaeologist who became the inspirational military liaison officer with the Arab Revolt against the Ottoman Empire, and thus became known as 'Lawrence of Arabia'.

Ludendorff, General Erich, 1865–1937 (*German*) Hindenburg's right-hand man during the war, serving with him on the Eastern Front and after 1916 as his Quartermaster General on the Western Front.

Maude, General Sir Frederick, 1864–1917 (*British*) The commander who restored British morale by the recapture of Kut in 1917 and whose forces took Baghdad the same year.

Moltke, General Count Helmuth, 1848–1916 (*German*) The nephew of the General who beat France in 1870; but his own attempt in 1914 to emulate his uncle failed and he retired.

Monash, General Sir John, 1865–1931 (*Australian*) Served with ANZAC forces throughout the war, ending up as commander of the Australian Corps in 1918.

Nivelle, General Robert, 1856–1921 (*French*) A successful French commander in Verdun in 1916, but his attempt at breakthrough as Commander-in-Chief in 1917 failed and he had to retire.

Pershing, General John, 1860–1948 (*American*) The commander of the successful American Expeditionary Force in France 1917–1918.

Petain, Marshal Philippe, 1856–1951 (*French*) Began the war as a Corps Commander, but his military skill as head of the Centre Army Group at Verdun in 1916 turned him into a hero. In 1917 he became the Commander-in-Chief of the whole French Army until the war ended.

Plumer, General Sir Herbert, 1857–1932 (*British*) Served as Commander of the Second Army in 1915, with a brief service on the Italian Front in 1917.

Putnik, Field Marshal Radomir, 1847–1917 (*Serbian*) The Chief of Staff of the Serbian Army until his death in 1917.

Rawlinson, General Sir Henry, 1864–1925 (*British*) Became Commander of the Fourth Army in 1915 and briefly at other times of the Second and Fifth Armies.

Rennenkampf, General Pavel von, 1854–1918 (*Russian*) In charge of the disastrous 1st Army in 1914.

Robertson, Field Marshal Sir William, 1860–1933

(*British*) Chief of the Imperial General Staff 1915–1918, known popularly as 'Wully'.

Rupprecht of Bavaria, Field Marshal Crown Prince, 1869–1955 (*German*) Commanded the 6th Army in 1914 and in 1916 a whole group of armies under his name. He would later have a strong anti-Nazi record.

Samsonov, General Alexander, 1849–1914 (*Russian*) In charge of the disastrous Russian 2nd Army in 1914, committing suicide on their defeat.

Townshend, General Sir Charles, 1861–1924 (*British*) The commander of the British/Indian force besieged at Kut in 1915–1916.

Wilson, Field Marshal Sir Henry, 1864–1922 (*British*) A Corps Commander who became Chief of the Imperial General Staff in 1918.

SELECTED BIBLIOGRAPHY

There must be thousands of books on the First World War. This one has been written in the Roskill Library of Churchill College Cambridge, which has several thousand on the subject. I have consulted more books than appear below, but many of them would now only be available in universities or specialist libraries.

The books chosen below do two things. Most of them cover the whole war, although I have chosen a few that specialise in a particular time or region. And the majority have appeared recently, so that anyone can buy them if interested – local libraries might have some of the older works but not others. There are also some very good online interactive maps. Some of the better ones are listed here.

Enjoy reading them.

Barnett, Correlli, *The Great War* (London, 2003)

Beaver, Patrick ed., *The Wipers Times* (London, 1973)

Hastings, Max, *Catastrophe* (London, 2013)

Holmes, Richard, *The Western Front* (London, 1999)

Howard, Michael, *The First World War* (Oxford, 2002)

Keegan, John, *The Face of Battle: A Study of Agincourt, Waterloo and the Somme* (London, 1976)

— —. *The First World War* (London, 1998)

— —. *First World War: An Illustrated History* (London, 2001)

Macmillan, Margaret, *The War That Ended Peace: How Europe Abandoned Peace for the First World War* (London, 2013)

Mallinson, Alan, *1914: Fight the Good Fight: Britain, the Army and the Coming of the First World War* (London, 2013)

Paxman, Jeremy, *Great Britain's Great War* (London, 2013)

Stevenson, David, *1914–1918: The History of the First World War* (London, 2004)

— —. *With Our Backs to the Wall* (London, 2011)

Animated Map: *The Western Front*, 1914–1918 BBC: [http://www.bbc.co.uk/history/interactive/animations/western_front/index_embed.shtml]

History of the First World War, 1914–1918 (WW1): [http://www.the-map-as-history.com/maps/6-first-world-war.php]

Maps & Battles, *The Great War*, Europe in 1914 PBS: [https://www.pbs.org/greatwar/maps/]

ACKNOWLEDGEMENTS

Most authors end their acknowledgements with a paean of thanks to their patient spouse. I think that it is better to start there rather than to finish, especially since my wife Paulette is the person without whom any of my books would ever get written. She is my constant muse and encouragement and my debt to her is always the deepest and the most profound.

This book began life in a Cambridge cafe, one that sadly no longer exists. It started as a conversation with the legendary Heffers' bookseller, Richard Reynolds, and Susie Dunlop, the publishing director at Allison & Busby. My thanks to both of them are very considerable and it is to them in particular that you owe the existence of this book.

Sadly, my normal mentor for works such as this, Richard Holmes (the military rather than the literary writer of that name), is no longer with us. What a wonderful encouragement he was to so many fellow historians, all much less well known than he was but whom he did so much to help and to enthuse. His daughter Jessica is still happily with us, though, as is a mutual friend, the spy-turned-historian Hugh Bicheno, whose knowledge of the details of many of the Western Front battles is magnificent. We all miss Richard but we hope that his life's work lives on in the continued interest in the story of World War I.

This book has been made possible by a three-year support grant from the Royal Literary Fund, to whose generosity I am more than grateful. (This is a personal rather than a project-related grant.) Eileen Gunn has been a pillar of support and helpfulness, and in conjunction with the Fund I am also very grateful to Hugh Bicheno, Nathan Buttery and Andrew Whittaker in helping to make the grant possible.

My mother, Elizabeth Catherwood, to whose uncle Harold this book is dedicated, has also been magnificently kind and supportive. Her parents were medical doctors and students during the war (she herself went on to survive the Blitz in a later conflict) and knew many who never made it home. Harold Lloyd-Jones was one of those who survived the horror of the trenches only to die in the influenza epidemic that swept the world when the fighting was over. His two younger brothers went on to great things, so who knows what he would have accomplished had he survived, like so many of his doomed generation.

Much of the research for this has taken place in the fabulous surroundings of the Churchill Archives Centre at Churchill College Cambridge. Winston Churchill played a unique role in the Great War, both as a leading politician, especially in his second post of Minister of Munitions, where his genius and support for technical innovation contributed enormously to the Allied victory in 1918. His time in the trenches, to atone for the strategic blunder of Gallipoli, gave him special insight into being a front-line soldier in modern war. To be able to write surrounded by the archives of such a man, and in the library of leading naval historian Stephen Roskill, which is situated in the Centre, is a rare privilege. Allen Packwood and his team have been the embodiment of enthusiasm and helpfulness to countless historians over many years and I am most grateful to them both individually and corporately. Thanks to Natalie Adams, Andrew Riley, Sophie Bridges, Katharine Thomson, Sarah Lewery, Julie Sanderson, Emily Morris, Gemma Cook, and Liz Yamada

My two Cambridge colleges, Churchill and St Edmund's, are great places in which to be based and I thank the Master and Fellows of both of them. Their Senior

Combination Rooms are each among the most convivial places in Cambridge, especially as their habitués believe in talking to one another in ways that are always fun and enlightening for all participants.

My writing is subsidised by my teaching for the Cambridge branch of the INSTEP programme. This brings the best and brightest students from select American universities (such as Tulane, Wake Forest, Villanova and sometimes others) to spend a term in Cambridge. Teaching keeps the mind alert and the fact that the students are a delight to be with makes the task all the better. The programme directors, Geoffrey Williams (the distinguished defence expert) and his wife Janice, are a joy to work with and I am as thankful to them for making this book possible as I am to many others.

As always I am indebted to Andrew and Clare Whittaker, Alasdair and Rachel Paine, Nathan and Debbie Buttery, Jonquil Drinkwater and Andrew Kearsley, Richard and Sally Reynolds, the Marshall family of Virginia in the USA and supportive friends of my wife such as Betsy Weaver Brandt and Gill Smith, for years of friendship and encouraging my morale as well as Paulette's.

My legendary agent Andrew Hayward was not directly involved in the commissioning of this particular book but his advice and kindness has always been indispensable.

My wife Dr Paulette Catherwood also gave a most helpful non-specialist's overview of the original manuscript, for which I am most grateful. She was helped by our delightful American god-daughter, Lauren Marshall, who kindly gave up some of her holiday from law school to give us her wise advice.

Warmest thanks also go to Sara Magness and Simon and Fliss Bage, the copy editors, who have done a superb job on the text. As always, of course, any mistakes remaining are mine not theirs.

CHRISTOPHER CATHERWOOD

CAMBRIDGE, 2014

To discover more great books and to
place an order visit our website at
www.allisonandbusby.com

Don't forget to sign up to our free newsletter at
www. allisonandbusby.com/newsletter
for latest releases, events and exclusive offers

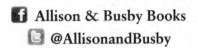

f **Allison & Busby Books**
t **@AllisonandBusby**

You can also call us on
020 7580 1080
for orders, queries
and reading recommendations